SPRING 59

A Journal Of

Archetype

and

Culture

Spring, 1996

SPRING PUBLICATIONS

WOODSTOCK, CONNECTICUT 06281

ACKNOWLEDGMENTS

To Princeton University Press for quotations from the *Collected Works (CW)* of C. G. Jung (Bollingen Series XX), translated by R. F. C. Hull, edited by H. Read, M. Fordham, G. Adler, and Wm. McGuire, and published in Great Britain by Routledge and Kegan Paul, London. Other quotations have been acknowledged throughout in appropriate notes and references.

Spring is printed in the United States of America, text on acid free paper.

Spring is the oldest Jungian journal in the world. It was founded in 1941 by the Analytical Psychology Club of New York. In 1970, James Hillman transferred its editing and publication to Zürich, Switzerland. From 1978 to 1988, it was edited in Dallas, Texas. Since 1988 it has been edited in Connecticut.

CONTENTS

[Because of the unusual length of this issue we have had to forego our usual Book Review section. It will resume in the next issue.]

SPRING 59: OPENING THE DREAMWAY

Wﾠhen Robert Duncan (1919-1988) chose the word "opening" for the title of his second talk at Buffalo, "Opening the Dreamway," he was using a word that had special, even *loaded*, connotations not only for himself but for several other poets in his group. The group, "the Black Mountain poets," as history has come to call them, was a major force in the poetry wars of the 1960s and 70s. They felt choked by the restrictive cultural poetics of the day, where poems were seen less as explorations than as finished literary masterpieces.

Their hero was William Carlos Williams (1883-1963), a pediatrician who spent his entire life delivering the babies of Paterson, New Jersey, (each one "a new beginning"), who wrote poems in his office in the few moments between patients. Hurriedly, but certainly not haphazardly, Williams' poems were the first breath of fresh air (the air of Paterson!) in what had become a programmed art form for academics and others prone to the formalities of the English literary tradition. Williams' gift to American writers was an unlocking of their own resources, the American landscape and language as Walt Whitman himself had left it for them. It was an imaginal landscape neglected for a century, as American writers expatriated to Europe.

The American poetry landscape could not have been more Anglified than it was in the 1950s, when Charles Olson (1910-1970) took over North Carolina's Black Mountain College and made it into a fierce training camp for a new generation of artists and writers. (See Martin Duberman, *Black Mountain: An Exploration in Community*, New York: Anchor/Doubleday, 1973). Along with Robert Creeley (1926-), Olson and Duncan became for awhile the dominant voices of their era.

One of Duncan's first books was called "The Opening of the Field" (1959) and the word appears again in the title of an essay on contemporary American poetry, "Towards an Open Universe." Olson had taught what he called "open composition" or "composition by field" (see his famous essay, "Projective Verse.")

These are poets for whom "opening" was everything, because everything, to them, felt so imaginally closed.

In taking on the "Dreamway" of Jungian psychology, Duncan was trying to open up some of the same rigidities of thought and practice there that poets had been challenging for years in their own domain. Not that the dreamway was not poetry's domain, too, but psychology was a field that, ever since Freud, had declared its own kind of ownership of dreams and fantasies, or at least of their interpretation. (You have only to recall how many dreambooks continue to be published, by Freudians and Jungians alike, in which symbols are actually listed, giving purportedly, their meanings! Psychology's programs were, and still are in their own way, as prescribed as poetry's.)

In opening the dreamway Duncan was challenging his audience to a free-wheeling exchange, from his perspective, on Jungian psychology itself. It is not easy reading, but not just because the lecture is a transcription rather than a written text. That fact obviously adds to the reader's difficulty sometimes, but it is Duncan's well-practiced ability to go with his own hesitations, to backtrack and spring forward in his thought at will, to range the field freely in the moment itself, that will give the reader pause. We hope you hear him out nonetheless, because we think these lectures are two of the most extraordinary contributions to archetypal psychology from the point of view of a poet that we have ever read.

Spring wants to take this opportunity especially to thank Robert Bertholf, Curator of the Poetry and Rare Books Collection at the Library of the State University of New York at Buffalo, for his kindness in making these lectures available to us and for his meticulousness in preparing the transcriptions themselves.

— *The Editors*

OPENING THE DREAMWAY

ROBERT DUNCAN

This lecture was given by Robert Duncan 14 April 1983 in Buffalo, New York sponsored by the Analytical Psychology Society of Western New York. The lecture was transcribed and edited by Robert J. Bertholf. The transcription attempts to represent the flow of Duncan's thought; in like manner, the punctuation attempts to translate the lecture from an oral presentation to a printed text. Duncan's mind worked very quickly, often with multiple frames of reference operating at the same time. Like anyone lecturing without a prepared text to read from, Duncan started sentences, dropped them, and began again. Some of these have been deleted. He also had the habit of combining vastly different ideas in the same sentence, and also in long runs of monologue. Mr. Bertholf has attempted to transcribe these as close to the oral text as possible. At times it was necessary to insert words to make the sense hold as a text for reading. These insertions appear in square brackets. Notes have been added as a way of clarifying allusions and references in the text. Printed with the permission of the Literary Estate of Robert Duncan. © The Literary Estate of Robert Duncan.

PAUL KUGLER[1]: "On behalf of the Analytical Psychology Society of Western New York and Hallwalls, I would like to welcome you here this evening. Tonight's speaker, Robert Duncan, has long been the center of the San Francisco Poetry Renaissance, and is, according to Kathleen Raine, the main visionary poet writing in America today.[2] By way of introduction, I would like to quote a passage from the preface to 'Prometheus Unbound.' There Shelley tells us:

> One great poet is a masterpiece of nature which another not only ought to study, but must study.

Duncan is just such a masterpiece of nature, a poet we must study. I have no problem stealing this from Duncan himself, from his 1965 introduction at Berkeley to Charles Olson, because it is Duncan who has taught us the importance of stealing from the Gods.[3] Here, then, is the master of The Truth and Life of Myth,[4] Robert Duncan."

As a prelude to my talk on things that I have found and questions that I have had in reading James Hillman, I want to read two examples, one long, [from] before I met or even had started reading James Hillman. I paid my $90, or whatever it was, because James Hillman was announced at the Jungian Center in San Francisco as giving a weekend on the un-

---

[1] Paul Kugler is a psychoanalyst practicing in Buffalo, New York. Hallwalls is an independent, alternative arts organization in Buffalo, founded in 1975.

[2] Kathleen (Jessie) Raine (1908-) is a British poet and scholar. She is the author of many books, including *Blake and Tradition* (Princeton: Princeton University Press, 1969) and *Yeats, the Tarot and the Golden Dawn* (Dublin: Dolmen Press, 1976). She is the founder of Enatharmon Press in London and the editor of *Temenos*, a journal devoted to mythopoetic literatures which has published thirteen issues through 1992.

[3] Charles Olson, "Reading at Berkeley 23 July 1963," in *Muthologos*, ed. George F. Butterick, vol. 1 (Bolinas, CA: Four Seasons Foundation, 1978), 97-156.

[4] Robert Duncan, *The Truth & Life of Myth: An Essay in Essential Autobiography* (New York: House of Books, Ltd., 1968).

derworld of the gods.[5] Before I even make another touch on that, I want to read a passage that is typical of my poetry. We are going to have to deal this evening with some questions and contrasts of a crisis in psychoanalysis, of which I know nothing, but it seems perfectly apparent that people are very uptight about it. And in our poetic illusion, we dream that patients go and deliver marvelous visions to psychoanalysts who turn around and know all about them; that's the one thing we are not permitted to do about our own poetry, but having them is our home fort. The more we know about our poetry, the more we're pushed out beyond it, because all that we know cancels out. So lore means clearly something different for the poet, but does it? That is my question. Reading the *Re-Visioning Psychology*,[6] I find something more important than anxiety. Something's happening in psychoanalysis where there were remarkable visions. In the first place, of course, Freud is primary as Hillman's new book opens up. His own identifications are always with the creators of story and the creators of image. He will identify with Leonardo. He will identify with Michelangelo and he knows the process through and through; and Hillman in his chapter in that book on Freud, locates an absolutely marvelous paragraph from an interview where Freud says: "I have always been misunderstood. Since I was a doctor, they have never read it right. I am actually writing stories. I am actually creating. I am not actually a doctor."

Freud and Dickens are the two things I read around the clock all the time. I have never thought I was in contact with a thing called psychoanalysis, because one of the best short story writers in the twentieth century [is] Freud in the things we call case histories. But the other thing that is striking to a poet is that Freud actually creates myth. I mean, where else can you ever find anywhere but in the imagination of Freud—and then in the imagination of us all, if we are responsive to the imagination—that putting out of the fire by pissing on it by the sons who have also

---

[5] Hillman delivered his lectures at the C. G. Jung Institute of San Francisco 11-13 May 1979. See James Hillman, *The Dream and the Underworld* (New York: Harper & Row Publishers, 1979).

[6] See James Hillman, *Re-Visioning Psychology* (New York: Harper & Row, Publishers, 1975).

killed the father in a primal scene. I am sure that one of the things that Freud thinks of being is Sherlock Holmes of 1900. Actually it is only A. Conan Doyle who is sort of a sensible detective because Sherlock Holmes is not to be trusted for birds, since he is making up the story.

Well, I will get to Homer before I thought I would get there. The character Freud is—at every point the anthropologist says, "no way." No way is there such a scene. Think about it, as a poet you have got a fat chance of ever having your creativity verified like this. The anthropologist says, "no way." Finally, psychoanalysis says, "no way." That is not what the story is. You're reading it literally, but Freud's telling it literally. Did you ever read a good story that wasn't literal? This is one of the battles of Hillman. Freud knows what did happen and he has absolutely nothing but the naked imagination to make such an assertion, and it is not made as an assertion, it is made as what you know that no one could possibly know, the one thing the imagination does. One of my troubles, always in the world, is that I only imagine. I did straighten out about believing and not believing; they must be alternate systems. Like you can't come and pee at the same time. So while you are imagining, you can't believe or disbelieve. They aren't in the same system at all, and I begin to realize more and more if that [is] the trouble Hillman has. He is wonderful at believing all sorts of things. But he does feel you can know and not know, which means you're coming from the wrong source, that imagination won't be there when you're knowing and not knowing. At one point, he says, he wants to have a poetic psychology. That seems to be hovering. Can we be poetic and direct? And he says I'm an agnostic. Well, you don't get to be a Gnostic or an agnostic. I am fascinated by Gnostics, but I realize that it isn't that I don't know, it is that I imagine and it crosses out all this business of knowing and not knowing. When you get news in the imagination, it doesn't bother do you know it or do not know it. There is no possibility of running around and checking out facts. And there are some sentences we will come to in Hillman where we find he is in that mode in the middle of his usual one, in which he is worried. He is more in Freud's hands than he would be in Jung's. Very close to Jung, who really is a master of what Freud can never understand, which is psychosis, what Hillman gives every evidence of is the one thing Freud did understand since he is a super neurotic, which is neurosis. All of his repressions and so forth show throughout Hillman's prose and we can't find one piece of evidence in all the writing. The really scary psychotic is the one who gives us no evidence of his psychosis anywhere. But there is lots of pressing, pressing, pressing of the kind of thing that Freud is so familiar with, and what conquers throughout—Freud then is the story-teller. It knows nothing of neurosis and psychosis. It is not mad, although Plato said poets are mad.

Poets have maybe been fighting, fighting, fighting to get in the story from the madness that was required of poets. The Greeks wanted that out of their poets very much. They wanted their poets still to be [a] shaman, and there is a line in which they had been, but that's not the one that comes in telling in Homer.

Now let me get around to the relation. The anthropologist just says about Freud's accounts, "no." The philosopher says, "no way." And psychiatry turns around and says, "well that's a little fantasy, local, of Freud's." He isn't talking about a fantasy he had, he isn't talking about something he knew or he didn't know. He talked right directly, like the storyteller knows that happened; and there is no possible substantiation in any direction that doesn't buzz the storyteller's signals.

Well, the effect was the same on Homer. When we turn around to the poetic field, we find myth we should rightly suspect is fiction, not myth. And the Greeks who took Muthos very seriously indeed, also had the idea that the actual knowledge of the gods and even the rumor of the gods that was in their mysteries, should never appear in poetry. A bit of my storytelling I will not substantiate by rushing through. The anxiety of Hillman to rush through and find—does some anthropologist, does somebody else know that this was it? Well, all of them are in the same place. The way I see it is that was always essentially the thing in Greece. Plato tells us, almost gives the mystery away, that Homer lied about Helen. But Euripides himself in opening his Helen will tell us that Plato lied about Helen. And Herodotus will give us historical reasons, I mean, that Homer lied about Helen. And he is

identified throughout [by] all of the people who start to talk
about mysteries. This is before Plutarch will say the mysteries
have broken down. Already they can spread the rumor about
whenever they have had a hint of what the mysteries were. That
means that we are not going to find them in Plato. That, as a matter of fact, the audience, the auditors, will rise and tear the person
apart. Our picture of the Dionysian fury is when the nature of
the divine is actually betrayed. So Plato is one of those great fic-
tions. And a cunning one indeed, because Plato is the one who
observes in the very first book that we know of at all as a book,
he observes that if philosophy were ever written down, it would
be turned into a fundamental law, into a problem of reading.
Well, what is in it? It is the very first philosophy ever to be written down. It is no longer a philosophy. Aristotle has to straighten
that out. And when you go to the actual dialogs themselves, you
find that you are in something like James Joyce, the cutting of the
puns, the cutting of changes of character. In a philosophy class
when it's taught, you are supposed to overlook that they are all
drunk at the end of the *Symposium*—totally out of their minds
drunk and groping each other, and far beyond that, they are going to sleep, snoring. As in *The Zohar*, none of it is dialectical in
that it never approaches a higher truth.[7] One story, all the stories
co-exist. So they are like *A Thousand and One Nights*.[8] They are
like *The Zohar*. One in the Persian world, in the Arabic world,
and another in the Jewish world of the thirteenth century, another one in the hands of Mr. Plato, who knows exactly what he
is saying. One thing you don't want at all in this state, which
would be a state that actually was discreet about the mysteries,
which is the essence of *The Republic*, you don't want the poet in
there. You don't want in this state the author of *The Republic*
himself.

Now, when you come to *The Laws*, he is already not wanting
himself in himself. That is a different trip. *The Laws* are in old

----

[7] See, for example: *The Zohar*, trans. Harry Sperling and Maurice Simon, 5 vols (New York: The Rebecca Bennett Publications, 1958).
[8] Commonly called "Tales of the Arabian Nights." A standard edition: *The Thousand and One Nights*, trans. Edward William Lane, ed. Stanley Lane-Poole, 4 vols. (London: Bell, 1906).

age, when he himself divorces himself from his creativity, and is alarmed. And one of the laws is that there will never again, there should never again be a *Symposium*, the one masterpiece in the center of it. And in a sense, of course, there shall be *Laws* and not *The Republic*, because *The Republic* and the *Symposium* belong to the cunning of the poetic mind. Previously we see a Parmenides who presents problems for philosophy that they can't ever cope with and previous to that, Heraclitus. All of them I read as poets in the same way as I read Nietzsche as a poet, not a philosopher.

Well, this is illustrating in a way. That a poet comes and reads [is part of] Hillman's crisis with psychology, and earnestly written, as far as I can figure out—certainly not the poet's in *Re-Visioning Psychology*. And throughout calls for two things: one is that there should be a poetic psychology. A poet would know that this is catastrophic; I mean, Plato knew that there better not be a poetic republic. A republic should have no author. It can have a counsel of philosophers or something, but it should have no author and meanwhile the work of *The Republic* has an author. And in a sense, one of Hillman's troubles is that he experiences Freud absolutely as an author. While Freud always identifies with the creative artist, Jung identifies with a Magus. And our difficulty and our necessary *politesse* about the Magus is that wherever you find the Magus, you only find him in the creations of art. When you look back to find the Zoroastrian Magus, you find him wherever he is found in the work of Shelley, and the work of Goethe. You realize that a poet is handing us this figure. So we've got Jung as the Magus, almost the reader of poetry. Remember that his first encounter of the word "Self" is when he is talking about a poem of Nietzsche's. He is not reading a poem of Nietzsche's as Magus or as Philosopher, he is reading him as a poet. There are very, very few; in all the works of Jung, there are very few resources ever taken in poetry. Quite rightly. So you don't find Rilke. When you come to a philosopher who we might indeed wonder, "Is he possibly a poet?", like Heidegger, that is out of bounds. As a matter of fact, Jung goes into a very personal rage and outrage at how come this audience is listening to this, he sees him as the contrary to the wise old man. He sees him as a stupid con man and suddenly he sees his German audience as taken in by this con. And there are no references to the contemporary poets; Jung knows nothing about them. Where he encounters works of art as with *Finnegan*[s *Wake*] or as with the [Picasso's] *Guernica*, we find that he does not see the order we see. *Guernica* is over-composed is my own response to it. He sees madness. Quite the contrary of what the artist knows is there. The artist's great question is, "Why isn't there madness?" *Guernica* is a grievous offense that supposedly you would never have composed. And we see over-composition in it.

The Magus that Jung is enamored of emerges over and over again—that determines what he looks for. It is the Magus and alchemy that he goes to. Whereas as artists, we see the drawing. We see the picture. We see scenes as in Shakespeare. The alchemical romance is way forward compared with the mysteries of alchemy, that the occult world as well as psychological world draws out of alchemy. We will be going toward it; because it is in his alchemy of elements that, it seems to me, Hillman does begin to make the transition to the poetic, and consequently crosses a border, so that all through *Re-Visioning Psychology* he's trying to evoke and trying to evade [a border] at the same time. And forces a horizon where it would appear, that is out beyond him and, like an hysteric, forces [a horizon] that will only appear when it will overwhelm him. In other words, he himself won't go into it, but it will tear him apart and open the way he has got to go.

[When the question of a title came up] I said, well, "Opening the Dreamway." The most striking thing to me is that it dawned on Hillman that we must open the dream to be its own realm, instead of ransacking in it. We can interpret it and so forth. There is no trouble there. We can tell stories about it, but the stories we have been telling about it must not come between us and its absolute experience. It is an experience, not a reflection. That is like an either/or. Hillman gets caught in the either/or, I just did. But it is when we say it's not only a mirror, it is also an absolute image. Pound very early said in "Imagism," an image is not a metaphor. And it dawned on all the Imagists and everything that is dreamed out of it. Yeats had already seen it, an image is not a symbol. Symbols are generated by images. Metaphors are generated by images. Our minds work with and create out of images, but images are absolutely there. We may have entities in our psyches that respond to it, and that's the nearest I come to the presentation of what is the archetypical in Jungian psychology. Yes, we must have an aptitude for the way, for one of the ways, at least, in which the image seems to overcome us, and swamp us, and haunt us, and not let us go. But that already tells us the image must be there, and when we come to poets, they will inhabit the image. They don't experience an archetype; they inhabit the image itself with no archetype in between at all. If you think about it in your Jungian terms, that great poet, Plato, was talking about an archetype of a chair, out of which all chairs flow. And that's one the artist understands. It does not pre-exist. It does not exist. It is imaginatively immediate and your chair is the place where it can be manifest, and until it's manifest, you are not in the presence of it. And it is hard to explain we're right at the very nest of the feeling of form, and that is one place where we have our actual mystery in poetry.

Working on the poetry of H.D. where the form is absolutely hallucinatory, the character we would think of as the numinous. I thought, could it really have to do [with the idea] that the whole universe is formal throughout at the subatomic level? It is always, what is the particle it all comes from? Well, now atoms, which were after all fairly rational propositions coming all the way from the Greeks to our contemporary period, have suddenly ceased to be the foundation and the foundation is the charm of poets. I keep thinking, "Who leaped poets into physics today?" And more than that, they are called quarks. And that is right out of Oz. I mean out of Oz. I mean science is way ahead of psychoanalysis to go dig the Oz books to come up for the foundation of everything. No trouble of fantasy at all in the science world. At all. But then they have never been blocked from seeing, re-seeing the absolute universe. And at the same time built into our contemporary science idea is, you never arrive at that actual universe. One fact perceived means the change of the whole fiction. You do not cling to a fiction so that imagination has to make a leap every time a fact enters. If the fact doesn't fit the fiction, only the imagination can now re-see the whole thing. So, this re-visioning is what has always been going on in physics.

But let me give you a hint that psychoanalysis may not be the only one in this feeling that you're in a crisis of re-visioning. The mathematician, Dirac, said, it is almost twenty years ago, since we no longer have anything but answers in mathematical physics we must be wrong.[9] It is only a question, it is only the question, not the answer at all. All you have to do to dissolve a question; and that is part of what I see working, working, working, can we dissolve every question we have and force a question [to] come at us, not out of us—that is what I see working in *Re-Visioning Psychology*. But it takes a mathematician to say, since we have only answers, and we can't picture a question, we must actually be wrong. That is deeper-going than could we re-vision it? Only because we have questions are we on the right path. And the minute you have an answer, then your path becomes extremely questionable in contemporary science. And the experience of it, by the way, is you just end up inventing atom bombs and useful things, and you are no longer confronted with the universe. This is one place that I find extremely weak throughout psychoanalysis; there is some picture that the body, the soul, the spirit, the "Ka," the "Ba," is not an absolute confrontation, child-of and confronted with the universe. For instance, around the Hellenistic Period, people no longer go to see where the sun is actually rising at the equinox. They had already discovered in Sumeria that there was a precession of the equinoxes. When the poet Chaucer says that the sun is in Aries in April, when it hasn't been in Aries for a thousand years by that time, that means astrology is entirely conventional and no one is in contact with the stars, except the ones who are still looking at the stars and still wondering about what in the world are the real patterns in what they are seeing. They extend into third, fourth, and so forth, dimensions. They begin to see that there are depths, when you get even close to that. It is not a mental idea. Some people experience it as alienating their soul from the universe. But what if you couldn't be alienated? Now your soul has extensions that go far beyond what you could be-

---

[9] Paul Adren Maurice Dirac (1902-1984) was a British mathematician known mainly for his work on quantum physics. His book *The Principles of Quantum Mechanics* (Oxford: The Clarendon Press, 1930) is a landmark publication on the topic. In 1933 he shared the Nobel Prize with Erwin Schrödinger.

lieve. And a person we don't usually think of as having an epiphany or soul or a spirit in his whole account, Bertrand Russell,
asked, "What is the miracle, what is the one miraculous?" And he
said, "Yes, when I was eighteen or nineteen I suddenly realized
that when I see a star, the light from the star, which is not only
millions or billions of years away, has across years and across
space, has actually entered my eye."[10] You don't just see a light, it
enters your eye. The Greeks were not wrong about that. It has
entered your eye. And the other one that makes it even more of a
miracle, is that in a whole apparatus, a mere mechanism, that is
recreated to belong to the brain's apprehension of what sight is.
Recreated in a way that is truly mysterious when you turn
around to these. I mean, you can draw the mechanism forever,
but the recreation is, indeed, a fantasy of the brain of how to read
light. We have some clinical cases where the light will be read as
sound, thought of as disorders by people who won't accept it.
Evidently it is widespread in children, so they are trained to be
ashamed by the fact that they see sounds. And at the same time,
poets bear witness over and over and over again that they are sur-
viving children where the experience of seeing sounds and hearing
light is so intense that it never leaves them. A whole population
does this, because the rarity of all of these things is how uniquely
and all alone each of us realizes or receives this. I mean, Bertrand
Russell is not telling my experience when he is saying that suddenly he realized that he can't look at the universe. Everywhere
that he even lets it in, it enters in. So we either do admit the universe or, at great cost, and we also do this by the way, try opening up to the universe. You can see I have a map here to talk
about Hillman and I open up and I am right in the box of the Hasidic Rabbi who, when asked by his followers, "Why don't you
write? You are wonderful, wonderful and you speak so marvel-
ously." He said, "But I have to tell you the minute I start speaking, the whole universe enters me and drowns me. And out of
that I speak, you want me to write?"

---

[10] Betrand Russell (1872-1970), British mathematician and philosopher. See his *The
Autobiography*, vol. 1, 1872-1914 (Boston: Little, Brown, 1967).

The person of Hillman is actually miraculous. And while it itself begs for profound experience, it itself recognizes itself as mercurial. I keep wondering, maybe these are false leads, but we experience it as, well, as Yeats would have said, maybe the mask is telling us I'm mercurial. We are not talking about psychology here, but poets deal with this first one who comes up, with the one who comes up into your play, not yet all talking about a psychology. Talking about the events that have to happen in the play, not the ones who have to happen for the sake of your soul at all. The persons who inhabit the play are not at all the same as the persons that inhabit whatever is the depth of your life, in writing. I think if I struck it, if you begin to hear me, I wouldn't have permission. When you strike the thing you are up against, and is essential in that way, you can no longer wear its costume and its mask. You hear flickers from Hillman all the time. It is not the one I wear and tell you I am. Actually the door. Actually the door I won't open. The door. And he has a fund of lore about this possibility. In *Re-Visioning* and in *The Dream and the Underworld*, he's still wondering, if I go to the underworld, will it open the door? And one of the things moving through the *Underworld* book itself and through *Re-Visioning* seems to be that he is locked out from pathology. He says that we have got to have pathology. Well, try that on. Lend that book, this book, that says we have locked out pathology to some cannibal or somebody right into the pathological. His pictures of the pathological, none of them relates to him. All of them are lists of court cases that we would view as possibly pathological, yet a novelist would know you wouldn't even experience them as pathological if you started into the core of the characters. Suddenly that is called life, not pathology. Pathology is a term that belongs to the world he wants to open. Imagine looking for the way out of where psychologizing is in time by looking for [what] the pathological is. Poets don't know what the pathological is. He does see the sociologists are first cousins here. They have their idea of the pathology and those are the windmills he contends against. Yet he wants a way out.

Well, I went to that weekend, no wonder I went to it. I want to just read here a passage that is from a poem of mine that I wrote

at the very beginning of the period that *In the Dark* belongs to. I
am not reading the whole poem at all, but I want to give you
what this is:

> this stealing of a life-fire,   of this
>   Promethean infancy,
> from the foundries of a parental embrace,
>   up from the debris of dreams
>   into the body desire prepared
> to rise again from its own ashes—
>
>   familiar,   strange,   familiar,
> just here,   this joyous quietude,
> already troubled by the falling away
>   of remnants of another life
>   into Lethe.
>   *
> I do not speak here of that river
> you read to be an allusion
> to ancient myth and poetry,
>   though it too belongs to a story,
>   but of a rushing underground in the very life-flow,
> a sinking -back,
>   a loss of the essential in the
> shadows and undertow —
>
> from which I come up into the day time.[11]

Well, one of the things we do in poetry is that when things occur in our poem, they awaken in us a set of signals of things we
have to be responsive to. Some three or four years after the writing of this poem, I knew if anybody's giving a weekend on the
non-Lethe, on the underground, I know I'm called to go. I would
point out the difficulty of the misunderstanding between poetry
and psychoanalysis, not for my soul's sake, but because the poem

---

[11]"The Quotidian," in Robert Duncan, *Ground Work II: In the Dark* (New York:
New Directions, 1987), 10-11.

demands it. And my soul would give up all of its life? No, I have another vow in that one, and a firm one. But it gives up all of its own possible existence to the poem. But if the poem were to intrude upon my household, I'd kick the muse in the face and throw her out of doors. I mean, at one point, Spicer,[12] who is dying and he wrote a note—we have not been speaking for years—and asked me to come and I went. And he said, I don't understand when you whore so much. That means I read to groups like this or talked and I got paid for it, so that makes it absolutely, if I'm paid for it, I'll do it kind of philosophy about truth. Why poetry comes to you again, I said, Spicer, in the beginning confronted the muse. And one of the great errors, by the way, that psychology makes, is to mix the Muse up with the anima. There is no such possibility at all. The muse is an absolute presentation. In the first place, she, it is no question about she. Try a male muse. There is an anthology of homoerotic poetry and Eros [that] shows strong signs like the Hebrew/Christian one does of almost exclusive homosexuality.[13] So, that as a matter of fact, by the time a novelist writes the story of Eros and Psyche, he is doing a rather astounding thing in the Hellenistic Period.[14] Within a hundred, within fifty years or something, you almost think it is as fast as Hollywood, within two years they've got altars all over the place. But Eros has changed his shape. He is no longer the scariest monster that ever came out in the first five as announced in poetry, but now announced in a novel, not a poem, but a novel. An entirely different kind of fiction. If Plato were the first in an absolute takeover of something you thought as philosophy that actually proves to be a kind of "poet-taken-over-the-book," that Appuleius would take over a novel transformed just

---

[12] Jack Spicer (1925-1965) was a friend and poetic ally of Robert Duncan beginning at Berkeley in 1946. Spicer, Duncan, and Robin Blaser began writing what is now known as "the serial poem." Spicer's poems are collected in *The Collected Books of Jack Spicer*, ed. Robin Blaser (Los Angeles: Black Sparrow Press, 1975).

[13] Ian Young, ed. *The Male Muse: A Gay Anthology* (Trumansburg, NY: The Crossing Press, 1973). Duncan's poems "Sonnet 1," "Such is the Sickness of Many a Good Thing," "5 Pieces," "Unkingd by Affection" appeared in the anthology.

[14] See Erich Neumann, *Amor and Psyche: The Psychic Development of the Feminine, A Commentary on the Tale by Apuleius*, trans. Ralph Manheim, Bollingen Series, no. 54 (Princeton: Princeton University Press, 1956).

out of romance into an actual novel, layered all the way though like James Joyce would do it, and an old lady tells us, an old crone tells a story. The woman, the wise woman, is always the woman who has passed through menopause and now sexuality belongs to her. No babies, no anything else. She is not going to be a mother. Her own sexuality is her own. And she suddenly becomes wise, where before she was, as a matter of fact, the worst of all of the fools of the world. The victim of every kind of thing. Her sexuality never belonged to her until she passes through menopause. Well it's one of those really old crones who passed through life so that menopause means nothing. At the end of life, you can dispose of life. Life is yours. Who cares if sex is yours? Life is now, and she tells this story, with all of the wonderful malice that life has toward its own transformations. Well, but it hit. It was the hit of the season. All the juke boxes were playing the tune and, lo and behold, they had altars and you would believe that Greece had always been praying. Jane Harrison will go back and look at vases with little figures flying out of the corn and try to relate them, and know she can't, to this story of Eros and Psyche.[15] But Eros had changed. He doesn't look like a monster. By the way, if you remember the story, the sisters and the parents tell Psyche, that is, indeed, you shouldn't have a thing to do with him. He is a monster, like we always knew. He hates love. Plato tells him, his mother is Need and he is the enemy of all decent human relations. Shall we take a survey of people having marital troubles? They must have written that into the myth in the first round. And Eros said, as a matter of fact, that you go through hell, literally, as Psyche does, to be united with him finally. And Aphrodite turns into the suddenly wicked beyond belief, although the Hellenistic Period had that strong belief only Athena is more scary. She is actually as scary as Yahweh.

Let me give you now a poem that directly relates to that weekend. I find about myself when I have a thrilling idea it has got to stop being present in the thrilling entirely. As I usually put it, all

---

[15] Duncan read and refers to two books by Jane Harrison (1850-1928): *Prolegomena to the Study of Greek Religion* (Cambridge: Cambridge University Press, 1903), and *Themis: A Study of the Social Origins of Greek Religion* (Cambridge: Cambridge University Press, 1912).

poetry comes from a rhythm and mine comes from dance
rhythms. You don't dance from your feet. You dance like a pup-
pet from your hands and your feet. Once it gets into my hands,
remember, the hand as the Balinese teach, is where you are dancing.[16] All the rest of the body is beautifully hung from this point,
the spine is and the torso and everything now moves from here.
But this is the same hand with which I write. Now cramped over
and carving and designing the letters, and my entire mind, which
is essential to the poem, is not at all concerned with the content
you hear. It is concerned with letters and phones, letters and
phones. That is what it is recognizing. Meanwhile there is a wonderful bit in the *Iliad*, when they try to win Achilles over to coming back into the war. They find him playing upon his formings
and ravishing his *psyche* and ravishing his *thumos*. *Thumos* gets left
out of contemporary psychological considerations, but that is
what he is doing. That is what a poem does. The sound gets to
you. And it says, and singing of and this would, of course, alarm
Hillman, of what of heroes and deeds. But the heroes and deeds
in the *Iliad* are hairy, scary. Hero is not a moral hero. It is the
hero which encounters the world and the hero who is encountering the world is not in any way encountering morality. That is
not what he is doing. He feels absolute. It does get mixed up with
his honor. I mean, there are certain places where you experience
what the world actually is. The way you stand in it. But we have
this ravishing picture; it is like that little picture of the poet [who]
knows about his audience. Their minds are filled with this movie
that rises of the events. They are re-seeing the movies; by the
way, they all know the events of the *Iliad*, they know many more
events than are there. Homer casually refers to events that the
Hellenistic Period tells us were there or weren't there. In several
places no one can find [if] there were ever such events. They can
be assumed. The audience is hearing eternal events, so, of course,
they all know them. But they are actually in a hypnagogic stupor
and their souls are ravished and raptured, raped. And their Thu-

---

16 In a lecture on H.D. at New College in San Francisco dated 21 January 1956,
Duncan refers to Antonin Artaud "le Théâtre Balinais," in Henri Cartier-Bresson's
book, *Danse a Bali* (Paris: Robert Delpire Editeur, 1954), 11-16.

mos is ravished and raptured, raped. I brought this subject up at a convention and several alarmed feminists, where it is a signal word, said, "How can you say that, rape and rapture?" I said, "Well, people experiencing rapture feel it as a violence against their soul and spirit." They don't feel just lifted. We've got figures over and over again of what a rapture is. Ask Ganymede, "Did you feel good when the claws were in you and off it went?" In Rembrandt's shocking literal painting, he had the genius to be literal.[17] There is also an assumption, by the way, in Hillman, that you can be merely literal. We artists know that the moment of being literal is out beyond your own talents and comes only by inspiration. Yet, eternally shocking is the literalness of Rembrandt's *Ganymede*. Where an absolute baby is pissing all over the lower part of the canvas and the eagle is dragging it away and the baby is in a thing that the Greeks understood rapture was. Or Persephone is in a rapture when she is carried off by Pluto and there are many figures of being carried off.

I was in Innsbruck and working with the *Theogony* of Hesiod and I already, a full year for sure after the weekend in the underground with James Hillman, evoking it throughout, by the way.[18] When he is actually speaking, we are in the part where he actually enters the domain of poetry. [He] becomes a kind of image in which we start going with what is going on in this speech. I found myself on Styx.

> And a tenth part of Okeanos is given to dark night
>   a tithe of the pure water   under   earth
> so that the clear fountains pour from rock face,
>   tears stream from the caverns and clefts,
>   down-running, carving woundrous ways in basalt resistance,
>   cutting deep as they go into layers of time-layerd
>   Gaia where She sleeps—

---

[17] The reference is to Rembrandt's painting, *The Abduction of Ganymede* (1635).

[18] Duncan taught at the Alpine Center for Poetry and Literature, a summer school at Innsbruck, Austria sponsored by the University of New Orleans, 30 July to 3 August 1979.

the cold water, the black rushing gleam, the
  moving down-rush, wash, gush out over
  bed-rock, toiling the boulders in flood,
  purling in deeps, broad flashing in falls—

And a tenth part of bright clear Okeanos
  his circulations—mists, rains, sheets, sheathes—
  lies in poisonous depths, the black water.

Styx this carver of caverns beneath us is.
Styx this black water, this down-pouring.

The well is deep. From its stillness
  the words our voices speak echo.
  Resonance follows resonance.
  Waves of this sounding come up to us.

  We draw the black water, pure and cold.
  The light of day is not as bright
  as this crystal flowing.

Three thousand years we have recited its virtue
  out of Hesiod.
                 Is it twenty-five thousand
since the ice withdrew from the lands and we
came forth from the realm of caverns where
the river beneath the earth we knew
  we go back to.

Styx pouring down in the spring from its glacial remove,
  from the black ice.

Fifty million years—from the beginning of what we are—
  we knew the depth of this well to be.

  Fifty million years deep —but our knowing deepens
  —time deepens—

                              this still water
          we thirst for   in dreams we dread.[19]

Knowing forces you out beyond. So at every step of what I
know, like since Hesiod we've named the Styx, and we know
there was a glacial river before, and that knowledge is both absolute and literal. When I open the *Scientific American*, the picture
of the underground river is entirely different. That is the same
thing as in poetry. Poets don't reiterate. The poet who rediscov-
ers the Styx has not finally discovered the Styx nor has he supplanted all the appearance of Styx in poetry. And that phenomenon is one of the very first. The up-to-date [poets] feel like
they've shed the poetry of the past, but poetry absolutely reads as
if it was a huge field of an existence. And poets, like Rilke, is the
one coming immediately to mind, say that there is only one
poem, which all write. This is another thing we find in *Re-
Visioning Psychology*, very troubling to Hillman, but it seems to
me that the minute we say there is only one, then there is a multitude. You do not have either/or, you have an also/and. There is
only one, and there are a multitude of identies. Always one, but
always. And there is not only Styx, I mean, there are a multitude
of other rivers. All with their own powers. But there is not only
one Styx in time because you will find every appearance of Styx is
absolute, haunts all the others as this poem, for instance, opens,
and it doesn't open that I am giving you Hesiod, it tells you that
if you have been there, that one co-exists with this one. Especially
in this one, because Charles Olson got me totally deranged, he
got me confused with the ocean he was looking out his window
was Okeanos. I had to turn my own head around after his death
to realize that Okeanos wasn't no ocean. That Hesiod made clear.
So I am in that way taking it literally. Charles thinks Okeanos is
an ocean, but instead of that I say, well, he wanted Okeanos to be
as big as an ocean because he was as big as he was. He must have
been right about it in some way. Absolutely. The ocean must
have been more like Okeanos than any river they ever saw at the
point in which the ocean got its Okeanos name. Yet, in its entire

---

[19] "Styx," *Ground Work II: In the Dark*, 37-38.

story, it was one of those rivers. In Hesiod one river doesn't do the trick.[20]

After finishing *Love's Body* Norman O. Brown went into a beautiful depression and in the midst of that produced a series of little versions, he called them an Ovid.[21] And all of them were absolutely visionary poetry. I wrote that he is now really in the dangerous territory where he has never been before. Because he is the one who knows. He never made much move toward getting them into print and soon was becoming an authority on Islam. Corbin being conveniently dead, you could start enrapturing yourself or what with detritus from Corbin. And so he gives lectures on Islam, alarming to the people who are actually in Islam, so he is a bit of a poet.[22] That's exactly where the poet is. Burkhardt said, that in his picture of history, there were only three great forces.[23] They were distressing to all us mild and sweet pacifists—if you noticed that about me—the men of war, the ones who make up wars out of anything. Not heroes, by the way. Always, I'm wondering. Hillman always sees the heroes as a do-gooder and he doesn't like do-gooders. But heroes aren't do-gooders. They have no moral character at all. They are heroes is what they are. Lo and behold, you start looking at them. They all look awful, before you turn around, and artists love it. They become subject matters. They love them in dramas and so forth because they sense this absoluteness of the hero. Ten million can die easy as pie and it makes sense in that domain. If you think about Apollo. Apollo is our tutelary demon, daemon, and at the same time a god. As a god, no one trusts gods. I think it is Patricia

---

20 See, for example, Charles Olson's poem beginning "out over the land skope view..." in Charles Olson, *The Maximus Poems*, ed. George F. Butterick (Berkeley: University of California Press, 1983), 296.

21 See Norman O. Brown, *Love's Body* (New York: Random House, 1966) and *Negations* (London: Allen Lane, 1968)

22 Henry Corbin wrote two books which influenced Charles Olson and Robert Duncan. See *Avicenna and the Visionary Recital*, trans. Willard R. Trask, Bollingen Foundation, no. 66 (New York: Pantheon Books, 1960) and *Spiritual Body and Celestial Earth: From Mazdean Iran to Shi'ite Iran*, trans. Nancy Pearson, Bollingen Foundation no. 91:2 (Princeton: Princeton University Press, 1977).

23 Jacob Burckhardt, *The Civilization of the Renaissance in Italy* (Vienna/New York: The Phaidon Press/Oxford University Press, 1937).

Berry who says something about the Greeks trusted gods or that they were like images.[24] No way, gods, when they come in the *Iliad* never wear their own faces. They walk in and look like your old aunt. They just take any guise because they are in the same position angels are. They have to take a guise, no matter what. But they are wild cheats and the Greeks know it. You could trust your grandfather, and he is a fool and he lies. But never, never, never, never, trust a god. They are very sneaky. So if you see an image, that's great, but what if it were actually the appearance of a god? Then never, just be only cunning and the god will beat you at it. Athena turns around and tells us in the *Odyssey*, tells Odysseus, "You think you can lie. You think you're cunning, but I am the great liar." As a matter of fact, we begin to suspect maybe Athena is telling our friend Homer, "You think you have the virtue of poets that you can make lies sound like the truth? But I'm standing right around here, boy, and I really know that you'll never recognize me as I come and go because I am a complete cheat." Also, she was a very fierce lady.

Let me get the little passage that I marked because it has to do with the real trouble. Hillman has become persuaded that Apollo is the god of his enemy in the intellectual mind. And so he reads him out all the time, like I don't want your brain trip and we want to get back to the soul or to depth. The god who was healing in his hand is the one who has disease in his hand. The one who has the disease, is the only one who can cure it. The one who cures it is the only one who has ever had the disease at all, and so the cure is the disease is one of the ways you read all that. And he can't name him. He says some gods, well, as far as I know, there is no such plural at all. I have never really come across that Hephaistos gave you the disease. The dreams might tell you what do you do with it. But Apollo is the god of plagues and death and war. That is the role of the bow. In this case, the healer is the poisoner. The healer is the one who shoots the arrow that hits him. Strangely turned around by Nietzsche and yet, in

---

[24] Patricia Berry edited *Fathers and Mothers: Five Papers on the Archetypal Backgrounds of Family Psychology* (Zürich, Switzerland: Spring Publications, 1973), and she published articles in *Spring*. James Hillman in *Re-Visioning Psychology* cites "On Reduction," *Spring : An Annual of Archetypal Psychology and Jungian Thought* (1973): 67-84.

an essay that always gets misread, I can remember from my teens, in quarrels with people who thought you voted for Dionysus against Apollo when Nietzsche is telling us you don't have Dionysus unless you have Apollo.[25] You don't have Apollo unless you have Dionysus. You have another phony baloney coming along the way. And that everybody has been reading it wrong. That, as a matter of fact, Dionysus is not Zeus—I'm talking about Nietzsche's vision—but is Apollo. And Apollo is not Apollo, but is a Dionysus. People go on and on with this. Would you choose one against another and one represents passion in the upper range. I am not going to trace in my mind where all of a sudden Apollo emerges, but the Hellenistic Period is one that begins to present Apollo as a *nous*. I always see nooses—n-o-o-s-e and indeed he is, but as the higher mind. Well, there is nothing actually that shoots more deadly than the upper mind. I am not going to put mine on. I mean the soul would quaver and die in its boots to have the deathly intentions of the upper intelligence [at work]. When the intelligence itself turns to population explosion, it knows that you should eliminate everybody. Now one of those moments, when my *nous*, my upper intelligence, I said, "How come we contribute to population control and to gun control?" I said, "Every family ought to have eight handy guns and after Christmas they are gone." If we had universal armaments, we wouldn't have to be troubled. I mean, because they always shoot all the kiddies. We'd have no trouble with population. We wouldn't worry about a pill. Look at the statistics, like the automobiles, most of them is the family that gets done in.

So, Hillman at that point cannot name who the god is, who has this awesome power. And very much, and rightly, he is telling us that isn't the disease divine. It is indeed. It has always been. He says, we are no longer in contact with the gods. Well, not only did I come from a family that for three generations has worshipped the gods, and worshipped as a matter of fact the Christos. They thought of Jesus as a teacher, like Buddha; they worshipped Jehovah in all of his terrible character. They didn't really know

---

25 Friedrich Wilhelm Nietzsche, *The Birth of Tragedy, and The Case of Wagner*, trans. with commentary Walter Kaufmann (New York: Vintage Books, 1967).

how terrible Athena, the despoiler of corpses on a battlefield, was. But they had no trouble at all about would you trust a god? There was also Jesus, the teacher, Buddha, the teacher. They never thought of Buddha as a god. Buddha stunk. And, they've got gods and demons. So I asked myself also, from *Re-Visioning Psychology*, who are the we who do not think in terms of the gods? Poets have consistently. All of those who stem from the work of Lawrence or Pound or H.D., but you could also stem from the pre-Raphaelites. Pope betrays that the gods and daemons are still there, but they belong to our realm of poetry.

Now, we're back at Burckhardt. He said that the hero was one of those three men who make history. The second one was the man of religion. And they all misunderstand each other. And the poet is the third, who makes the whole character of men's essential and vital history. "Oh, wow! I'll memorize that forever," I said as an infant poet. And then I looked and read the next paragraph. He said they all need a certain amount of politeness toward each other because the man of religion thinks that poetry is a wonderful way to present and make persuasive the world of the divine, which is in the hands of the religion. And the poet thinks, "Wow! religion is filled with all the things I need to juice up my poem."

After all, poets when they see a mountain, they see it in a poem already. The more awesome it is, the more it flows out and is made for the purpose of the poem. This is one of the ones that is a speculation. Hillman sees almost in the Protestant theological sense, and certainly very much at this point in the Judeo-Christian sense, that you must be soulless if you do not live by the soul. Actually, the Greeks didn't believe that, at all. Your soul would be there in the precinct of the god, when you attended the god. And psyche was actually—and anyway psyche was—very visibly experienced in the body, as in movements in the body, movements from the body and so forth. But once soul appears on the scene, there is just one person who really wants it to be there, which is religion. Because they are the leaders of souls. When

souls appear in the *Works and Days*,[26] they sounded like bats. I
don't think that's what Hillman's talking about. And they are
flapping away. They're flapping away. I have a passage in
"Passages" and that is the place where I thought I saw the soul,
indeed.[27] So, I actually do experience soul as being very much as
the poets experienced it in Greece. As a matter of fact, little tiny
shadows, to use your Jungian observation on what the shadow is.
That is the inhabitants of the shadow. And they chitter and they
are robbed totally of language. They chitter away and fly off into
a sort of dementia to the underworld where they go to a grey
shadow realm. And below that is the great darkness in which
there is no shadow possible, which is Tartarus. Zeus in the *Iliad*
displays his power, extends in all these realms. There are four of
them. From the light in which there is no possibility of a shadow,
as a matter of fact, there is no possibility of lighting or of anything being lit. No image can appear in it. Through the higher
realms where the gods dwell. I am going back and forth, is the
Ether of Olympus, but there is a realm of a higher Ether that is
absolute, absolute pure light. And then the realm of shadows
where the after-death, underground realm [lies]. And in a way the
underground is also literal. It is the area you can see in the cave.
And it is a grey, shady place. Cold. Absolutely cold. And then
below that is abysmal darkness in which there could be no
shadow and, consequently, no souls. No seeing, no seeing at all.
And the one place I hear a description of it, because I think you
begin to hear that I have no division in my mind at all that sets
apart into contest, the psychic, or the intellect, or the physical. I
am struck by the fact that when they describe what happens to all
animal life when there is an earthquake above an 8.5 you lose not
only sense of orientation, but you can't tell if it is dark or light.
You lost that tropism. We can only think of dark. Yet, the description of it is you don't know whether it is dark or light. You

---

[26] See, for example: Hesiod, *The Works and Days. Theogony. The Shield of Herakles*,
trans. Richmond Lattimore (Ann Arbor: University of Michigan Press, 1959).
[27] "The Passages Poems" constitute a serial poem by Robert Duncan in multiple
parts. The poem entitled "Whose" has the dedication: "[for Jim Hillman's/ tribute to
Henri Corbin/ *The Thought of the Heart*," in *Groundwork II: In the Dark*, 81-82.

were completely, truly, disoriented in all the tropisms that keep you in the very beginning of your identity.

Hillman goes into a passage of Keats.[28] He only selectively quotes the passage and soon deserts the poem. He says, but we psychologists have to be more precise than the poet is and the poet actually is extremely precise. It is necessary for Hillman himself to misread key words through the Keats in order to become "precise" so that it will become psychology. There is no way it could belong to psychology had he paid attention to what Keats is saying. But he's filtering. He wants Keats to be psycho-pompous, psycho-pomp, but he doesn't. So he immediately says, "But I'm not going to go to the psycho-pomp, poets aren't precise." Along with Hillman I was reading Bachelard, and Bachelard, once says, "But I'm becoming precise and that destroys the archetype."[29] I began to wonder, "Does Hillman want to destroy the archetype?" Images don't arise, new persons don't arise, and the most alarming thing in the description—Keats arises with the idea that there is initially an intelligence and it has no soul because it will only make soul in the degree to which it discovers itself anew in the world, itself. And he doesn't mean some other world, he comes up against the world. We are very careless of the world. Mostly, if it doesn't hit us, we're not about to look into it. I mean we like to flow through it. But the one who flows through it now is not the soul at all. The one who floats through it is the intellect. It comes up against it and it starts to make soul because all of its life wounds are actual contacts with the one who makes soul. Keats says the use of the world is soul-making. Now, hurriedly, Hillman has to transfer that and this doesn't mean this world? Well, he has to throw away all the rest of three pages that Keats writes in order to say that because he is talking about this world. The chairs you're sitting on make soul if you even allow their existence. You now have something because the image also is there. If the image is only in a dream, you have to start to con-

---

[28] In *Re-Visioning Psychology*, Hillman cites Keats' letter of April 1819, ix and 231.

[29] In *Re-Visioning Psychology*, Hillman cites Gaston Bachelard, *The Poetic Reverie*, trans. D. Russell (Boston: Beacon Press, 1971). Duncan also read Gaston Bachelard, *The Poetics of Space*, trans. Maria Jolas, foreword by Etienne Gilson (New York: Orion Press, 1964).

nect with the image because it is everywhere. This is after all always the structure my grandmother talked about. Is my grandmother an anima? No, she's that invaluable fairy tale grandmother who knew everything and was an elder in the mysteries.
But poetry can continue the wonderful tit as Keats says. Or did
they pronounce it "teat." Poetry continuously sucks at the world.
It is not called the soul, because the soul is a process of making
and is then created.

While I looked at another term that was in Hillman, which is a
battle he has against the humane, the human. We've had enough
of the human and humane. I thought, "Oh my God, as a student
of Medieval and Renaissance history, there is nothing more in-
humane than the Renaissance where the humane made its appearance." The world still fascinates me, but it would be [a] vast relief
to drop way from the horrible inhumanity that surrounds me in
every corner. It is like Olson in the middle of that drunken dis-
play of himself at Berkeley said, we have had enough of beauty. [30]
I thought, "My God, in the first place, the auditorium we're sitting in is aggressively ugly. Exactly one of the most tremendous
creations of ugliness." It dawned in my little head that it takes just
as much creative energy to make mediocrity and make ugliness as
it does to make beauty and they aren't in the contest. If I want
some beauty around, then I got to make it where it is, but it ain't
gonna win. You don't make beauty because it is gonna win. It
isn't in a contest at all. You make it in order for it to exist at all. I
mean we love the transformation of the ugly into the beautiful,
but the ugly people don't love it. They are out with the police the
minute you make a good collage. To them, it seems as if you'd
said something about them.

Let's recall the work on Pan, which is one of the wonderful
roles that Hillman has that is extremely important to poets, that
is, because he exhausts the lore. He has poured forth into psychoanalysis wonderful concentrations of lore. Lore that exceed the
purpose of pointing something out. Along the way, of course, he
will recall that he is supposed to be pointing something out, and
points it, but mostly he loves, actually loves, as a poet loves, the

---

[30] See note number 4.

lore of the gods, the lore, now in the most remarkable pieces, of the elements. And one of the ones he approached, and he just had to join in his work on Pan with Roscher and himself, to a twentieth century wonderful accumulation and speculation upon Pan.[31] The very thing that I would read that personifying is an important section of, the beginning of the kind of work and process that Hillman is suggesting, a kind of alchemy beyond alchemy. The first one is to personify; that opens the door of what possibly can happen. Well, it is a misunderstanding to think that poets personify, but I can give you a point at which it became absolutely a crux. The poet Dante rescued, by making poets insincere, by telling the whole Catholic world that if it appears in a poem, it is a device of the poet. He rescued us from being burnt. In the *Vita Nuova*, in a poem that has to be testimony of a primal presentation, an angel, the angel Amor. Now, this is an angel that had been created, called into being. So that is creation in the most profound sense, in a circle of Cino, Dante, a circle of poets. They knew that this was extremely dangerous. You could search every resource of the church, and we did not find the angel Amor. Amor is not Eros. Amor is not amour. Amor may be latent, but it was not yet there in the troubadours. And Amor comes forward. And comes in a dream. So Dante tells us in all the sincerity of poetry that we can't doubt, because it is the imagination, that in a dream, now it means it came before, but is also testimony. That is the most important level, of all, to distinguish in a poem when you know it is testimony. And he says that angel Amor came with his heart, Dante's own heart, burning in the angel's hand and demanded that I eat of the heart. Now he doesn't make moral conclusions. He doesn't make psychoanalytic depths out of this. An image does not have depth. The minute an image has depth, it is a metaphor and you have left the image. The image is where it is, when it is, incognizant absolutely of depth. Won't

---

[31] See Wilhelm Heinrich Roscher (1845-1923), *Pan and the Nightmare:* being the Only English Translation (from the German by A. V. O'Brien, M.D.) of *Ephialtes: A Pathological-Mythological Treatise on the Nightmare in Classical Antiquity* by Wilhelm Heinrich Roscher; together with *An Essay on Pan, serving as a Psychological Introduction to Roscher's Ephialtes* by James Hillman, Dunquin Series 4 (Irving, Texas: Spring Publications, 1979).

lead you down. But images in Dante's world stand so absolutely
they are the very moment they appear and they are the very
place. That is the divine place in Dante's so they can't go up or
down. The poet does a very strange thing, a shaman-like trip going up and down, but that's one thing angels can't do. Okay, this
Amor is right there. Later in Dante's life he writes the *Convivio*
and he is being read now widely. He tells us in the *Convivio* the
gods, when they appear in the poetry of the classical world, or
the pagan world, are not at all real, they are metaphors. How
strange, where at the very edge of what, where Hillman wants to
continue that maybe the image would be saved if it were a metaphor. If it could lead him somewhere else. Up, down, over, under, but not to be where it is. Well, [Dante] says, "Yes." They are
devices and he proceeds to quote Ovid and a whole series and says
that these are not gods and we know they aren't, they are devices.
Then he turns on his own testimony and says, and that angel in
that poem is a device. Well, within a century of Dante, Joan will
be burned for talking to angels and to Our Lady. I [found from]
reading, Corbin—Islam goes to war against the angels and burns
people for speaking with angels. All congress with angels is broken in the fourteenth century. By the time you come past the
Renaissance you have got little wagons and little white suits for
you when you talk to angels. Only the Jewish community kept
talking to their maggids all the way through the eighteenth century.[32] And by that time, all of Europe and all of Islam felt that
angels were really a kind of perspective, as Hillman would say.
Not actually there at all, and no one in their right mind would
ever talk to one. And if it talked back, it must be that you are
having a little interior conversation with yourself. Now you've
got depth because you have a room in which two persons are,
who are both really you. Okay, and then we can trace through
that whole story of lunatics, people who talk to themselves. I
think that you can hear that, I can remember an aunt who was
really worried about bathrooms and I guess *Portnoy's Complaint*,

---

[32] Maggid, an inspirational and at times mystical teacher. The "Great Maggid of
Meseritz," one of the followers of the Hasidic leader Baal Shem, was such a teacher.
See Gershom G. Scholem, *Major Trends in Jewish Mysticism* (New York: Schocken
Books, 1961), 334-343.

had occurred to her and it hadn't occurred to me.[33] I was in a conversation with interesting persons who were in the bathroom. And in sort of bliss, talking back and forth. And suddenly an irate, very suspicious, Portnoy's mama starts banging on the bathroom door saying, "What are you doing in there? Are you talking to yourself?" I realized that this was the worst thing in the world to happen. "Oh, no, no, I won't! never again." Also, I never turned out to be a dramatist. Goethe tells us that his whole world emerged by talking to himself, lo and behold, and didn't dream it was himself. As Hillman begins, Jung would talk about the little people. Except in Jung there's a hint that the little people really are proper. We're on a threshold and that's the threshold Hillman, I think, wants to break through. He is blind to the fact that there are people who worship the gods. "Are you talking to yourself," was not what my aunt thought. "What little demons do you have in there that you are talking to?" Very early we were told if you're in a seance, if they come from over there, even if they don't lie, they really aren't any smarter than human beings. And you know how you wouldn't really trust anything a human being would say. I didn't know that was exactly how the Greeks felt about the whole question. And that will extend all the way through to Yahweh, Christos and so forth. Be careful, Christos will wipe you out. But he doesn't say we shouldn't think of Christos or dwell in the Christos, or as in my case, come as a matter of fact to have a Christos as a center, which is another strange allegiance in the line of the poem. How come among thousands, you were the one? That is an experience which doesn't say anything about: did you vote for it? That is as absolute as falling in love with somebody and there are eighty thousand people who look better or who would have been more jolly and so forth. But, there you are. Stuck, falling in love.

Let me give you this passage here where Pan appears. Let's say the thing I want to go toward now: Is Hillman also restraining himself from having rhyme, sound, and rhythm enter? And very striking for our anima. It was almost immediate contrast between Pat Berry, and you know how I read. She is giving her lecture in

---

[33] Philip Roth, *Portnoy's Complaint* (New York: Random House, 1969).

quotes and she had a flowing rhythm all the way through and her body was in it so things came up as much here in this world of the body. Her body is in it totally. And the rhythm told you a lot about what and where I think you hear a little about divine presences are in a place. If I move over here, I am in another place, so I don't have to ask, the thing on my mind will be here. That's how Greeks wrote poetry. They went back and forth, this way and then they turned around and went this way. And they were moving in between worlds because they were "wheres," places, absolute places, absolute places the body knew and the body was the magic agency, because place and time are the actual measure in which the divine talks, appears and so forth. It's always, then, in a place.

Today belongs to you, to the music
about to be heard, the distant luring call recalld,
the strain, the estrangement from all I knew,
another knowledge straining to be free.

O deepest Unrest, indelibly engraved in me,
the wilderness beyond the edge of town, the riverbottom road,
the lingering, the wandering, the going astray,
to find some wanton promise the derelict landscape most
    portrayd in me,
the fog's sad density of cold,
in me, the solitary and deserted paths
in me, the marshy wastes, the levee road
where day after day as if driven by the wind
I impatient strode, day driven after day,
until the rush of impending weather was most me
in me, the dumb about-to-be, the country way
incapable of speech driven toward impending speech.

I was never there. He was never there.
In some clearing before I reacht it
or after I was gone, some *he*
had laid him down to sleep where Pan
under his winter sun had roused the wildness with his song,

and, long lingering,
the air was heavy with his absence there—

Lord of the Heat of Noon still palpable
where late shadows chill the dreaming land.[34]

   In poetry at least, the appearance of persons and of images takes
place in a context of arousal that is not caused by the language,
but mounts as the language is aroused and doesn't come from that
arousal. The arousal of the language is the arousal of persons and
images. The prime level we can find in prose works. One of the
best examples I used to love is in Sapir's book on language.[35]
When he is aroused, suddenly, for four or five passages, not only
is the rhythm there, but the rhyme. Full rhymes fall into place.
Now the whole thing becomes evocative. Images rise. He imagines what language is and we find absolutely astounding statements that we aren't going to find anywhere else that tell us
about language in a way that linguistics has no right to tell us
about language. Coming up in a text because he himself is never
going to recognize what it was that moved him. D. H. Lawrence
writing a novel sweeps us on. As they sweep on and are aroused,
they not only are aroused into a passional state, they enter a passion of language itself, which is actually the threshold of the divine and of the person as such. If you have drawn away from persons, and you yourself have no yearning, no passional relation,
there is gonna be no passion in your prose. Persons will be a job
of describing them, little buttons, and white hair and so forth.
The typical metonymic novel is one in which there is no passional relation to the whole thing. So we find ourselves filling it
in and it is very much like the portrait painter who literally
paints the portrait. Not because no passion intrudes, but since
reality is only experienced to the degree that there is no passion
present, and the minute passion is present, the person working
experiences a distortion of reality. Lo and behold, we get this,

---

[34] *Ground Work I: Before the War* (New York: New Directions, 1984), "*Poems from
the Margins of Thom's Moly,* preface to the Suite," 63-64.
[35] Edward Sapir, *Language: An Introduction to the Study of Speech* (New York: Harcourt Brace Jovanovich, 1949)

what we call, in another sense, literal drawing. Literal account. Literal accounting for every detail, as if you built up things like that. Well, there we don't meet persons. We meet reconstructions. Even the term "re-visioning" is interesting. We love it because of the play on re-vision. Yet, this return is not the experience in which we actually encounter persons. We tend to the persons closest to us. To suddenly be surprised and realize that for months we have not been essentially looking at them. Yet if we were to draw them—I'm thinking of Jess. Draw a picture of him and you find, what is that face? Because we very quickly sketch in the people and they belong to our emotions and they belong to our affections, so we really don't allow anything to enter that is not in that frame. But we read it so satisfactorily that we've given it depth. All of a sudden it has no depth at all. It is there. Immediate. Now you have got the person. Now, you've got another thing that Hillman evokes throughout: the alien. Now, it is most remarkable. He feels it as a need to come into the alien. It is repeated throughout, a yearning. Hillman is in an entirely personal trouble here. This will not change the nature of the fact that there is a need. An entirely personal need. With Hillman, his perturbance of soul, another thing he evokes in this, actually is ours. And potentially we may suddenly see, not the Hillman we read, the Hillman we take to be Hillman, when we may see, as I said, the sudden Jess you see and you had never seen that face before. And you have been living with him for thirty years. And these are startling things to break through that show how much we give depth and psychological quality to things that actually have been right immediate all the time. And people, in order to live together, live on a kind of magic in which seeing and not seeing forms another threshold, called a tolerance in some sense, a neutrality in which we have our affections. And with increasing dread, what happens if I see. What happens if I am seen.

Let me give an example. Cocteau actually looked in a mirror; that is more than what we hear of in Narcissus. Narcissus discovered the space in which the world exists by looking into seeing. One of the strange things is Pat Berry talking about echoes. All of them trying to relate Echo, but Jess in his huge *Narkissos* canvas sees Narcissus as looking into seeing, and that is the area of the

visible world.[36] We mind everything about Narcissus. Some marvelous things are in Proclus's notes on Euclid.[37] If you think
about it of course, it would come up in Euclid. In the Gnostic
version, as far as Narcissus sees is the area in which creation can
take place. He sees into the seeable. The seeable is created by his
seeing and that is what he sees below. The eyes are enamored of
seeing. And Echo throws herself into sound. So we have all the
sound and sight of the world proposed in this myth. And in this
huge canvas you don't miss it. Echo is all of space and almost
bouncing into form after form after form after form. Falling into
sound as she leaps. Remember in the myth, she leaps from the
place where all things echo into that space. His sight falls to the
absolute boundaries of sight. And certainly the Gnostics felt that
that was going on all the time. Echo, no matter how far she fell,
the falling is stronger than where she fell. So, it works throughout
time. Her fall never stops. The end of hearing is not the end of
hearing. Because the fall itself opens up new doorways to dream,
to dreamways. And the same with Narcissus's sight and we see it
in science throughout. The conventions of the Hellenistic period
were not to see to the end of seeing, so they built very strong
conventions, seeing laws into astrology, catastrophically, because
after the Hellenistic period, the astronomer and astrologer were
identical. And the one thing we see in the theater of chemistry in
the seventeenth century is that men had now stopped looking
into the mineral world and seeing it as absolute and reading what
went there, and it turns into a convention, and turns into the stories that we have that come out of the lore about minerals.[38] The
lore about minerals, including a scientific lore, when it sets up a
lore of its own, lures us away and finally Hillman is pointing out,
but this is actually not sulfur. Then what will sulfur do? Jung is
marvelous on this, this is one place where reading Jung, when I
was in my teens and so forth, his first encounter with alchemy,

---

[36] Jess' drawing *Narkissos* (1976/1991) is the last picture in his *Translations* series.

[37] Proclus (ca. 410-485), *A Commentary on the First Book of Euclid's Elements*, trans.
with Introduction and Notes by Glenn R. Morrow (Princeton: Princeton University
Press, 1970).

[38] Duncan is referring to the great collection of alchemical writing entitled *Theatrium
Chemicum Britannicum* (1652).

he saw it.[39] You know, they must have actually been in a conversation with metal, but the thing I see in Jungianism is that they're in a conversation with metals, they're in conversation with Jung's portrayal of alchemy. And so is alchemy already in conversation with the theater of alchemy. The chemist is breaking away in the seventeenth century. It was no longer proper to talk with metals. So in the field of mystical alchemy it had become a metaphor. In the field of practical alchemy—the two couldn't have been separated before—there was nothing there to talk with. So when our friends, who invented the atom bomb, in their minds they weren't doing anything but defeating the enemy. They weren't in a conversation. You wanted to ask, if you were dreaming? What did you mean. If this had happened in a dream, what would be going on? But the other thing is, how could you not be dreaming? And we separate dream off from the day. Although certainly the message in Freud with the *Psychopathology of Everyday Life* and following *The Interpretation of Dreams* is that they were two fields of things happening and you couldn't really divide them. You couldn't say one was psychic and belonged to the soul and the other was practical and belonged to the body.[40] Freud could see that indeed the dream belonged to the body. The body suffered the dream as much as the soul ever did. The body's changed by dreaming. The body's messages flowed through dreaming as well as the soul's, as well as the spirit's. When he talks about pathologizing again, it does take us back to that title of *The Psychopathology of Everyday Life*. It may be to open up the actual. But even the dream is actual. "I actually dreamt it," "I didn't dream it," and so forth. "I made it up." "I made the dream up." All of those are dimensions of dream experience. "I am not sure if I did" or so forth.

---

[39] C. G. Jung, *Psychology and Alchemy*, trans. R. F. C. Hull, vol. 12. *The Collected Works of C. G. Jung*, Bollington Series no. 20 (Princeton; Princeton University Press, 1953).

[40] Sigmund Freud, *The Psychopathology of Everyday Life*, trans. James Strachey, in Collaboration with Anna Freud, assisted by Alix Strachy and Alan Tyson. *The Complete Psychological Works of Sigmund Freud*, vol 6 (London: The Hogarth Press and the Institute of Psychoanalysis, 1960); and *The Interpretation of Dreams* trans. James Strachey, in Collaboration with Anna Freud, assisted by Alix Strachy and Alan Tyson. *The Complete Psychological Works of Sigmund Freud*, vol. 4 and vol. 5 (London: The Hogarth Press and the Institute of Psychoanalysis, 1953).

And the day is the same way. "Yesterday I'm not sure if I did so and so." "I made up yesterday, but I don't know what it was." "I actually." All of those are stages of the way and if you think of these as ways and think of them as co-existent ways. Now thinking about music. These co-existent ways I think are something that I don't detect that much in the Greek world. As music begins to emerge in the Hellenistic world, but especially when our polyphony begins to appear and parts of the melody that was moving through a logical kind of time, that is, the unidirectional time, suddenly assemble in the chords and are heard in an immediacy, which may very well be one of the daring appearances in the art of the angels. I realize they belong to a figure, but you weren't in contact with it. But when the chord comes, think about a discord appearing, not in the distribution of a melody, but appearing, planning. We feel it as a force, which shakes body, soul. Ficino knows very well that the poem by its sounds, not by its myth, not by the muthos, by its sounds it reaches the soul, the body and the spirit.[41] The body cringes, feels immediately the sound and tone and distribution of notes toward possible resolutions, toward irresolution and toward awakened conflict.

For the last fifteen minutes here, I want to read "Alchemical Blue," which seems to me, as I said, the place where I find my goodness, aren't you in trouble, Hillman, because you have entered very close to the poem in what you are doing? And still are in your love of gathering lore. So lore, when you are just gathering it, as poets also gather it, is very different from when you are suddenly turning and start evoking all the lore in a rhythm and now out of that an emptiness appears in the whole lore. Not what you know at all, but the minute there is an empty place, the spirit, and soul and body, a new one will inhabit that place. The divine god would be present in the stone and would be present in the voice. The art of the poem is that the god appears. The content that we call the content is the body of the god. The sounds are the place where the god hides and that is the physical body.

---

[41] Marsilio Ficino (1433-1499) is mentioned by Hillman in *Re-Visioning Psychology*, 200. See Ficino, *Commentary on Plato's Symposium*, trans. Sears Reynolds Jayne (Columbia, MO: University of Missouri Press, 1944).

The content I guess could be called the soul and spirit, and these have been broken in the contemporary poet. Hillman's very aware of this. We've got a lot of poetry, for instance, which divorces these elements completely. And yet, to him, it always suggests that the poem has lost depth. I don't experience the body as deeper, as a depth below the soul, or the soul as a depth or being above or the spirit being above. He is very convinced that the spirit is superior, but that is only in certain frameworks. In the world, actually I thought spirit was like a little fire inside every cell. Well, how am I gonna decide the spirit is superior to something? It is absolutely part of the secret of the thing we call body. The body is itself part of the secret of the spirit. You know, no wick, no fire. Okay, this is one where I had dreamt for a long time and actually researched and exhausted the lore. It was the last piece to come into shape missing from a poem that is not at the end of that *Ground Work I* that has to do with *Before the War*. The deepest war. The most striking thing to me is that all of our wars are actually fake and they are not *the war*. Everybody knows that we know there must be a war and they are fighting all sorts of substitutes. And so gaily over a substitute over nothing. They will exterminate several million people. Then we know that's scarier than would you wickedly do it. The great problem for me is which is scarier? Hitler, who we know was mad. We have all sorts of evidence. Let's think of him as we think of him or as the Jews saw him, as the hammer of God, as he is actually the wrath of Jehovah, which is the mad part of the Jehovah. If indeed he is that, is he scarier than Roosevelt, who was a rational man and planned the bombing of Dresden because it was a non-military target and a cultural center and would break the German's spirit? Hitler was himself defiling and breaking the German spirit. If Roosevelt had been mad, it would be understandable. The madness is broken up, but what about if Roosevelt had been sane? I can't decide between the two. Is it more appalling to have this sort of thing come out of a sane and rational man or have it come out of history's madman who moved like hammers of God across history? I dare to dissent to that, but in *The Zohar*, which was written in the thirteenth century in Spain and is a devout Jewish work of the mystical world of Jewry, suddenly there is a shocking passage. The Rabbis are discussing, well, what will happen to the Jews who break even a bit of the law? And the inspired Rabbi says, "Oh, but God will burn them forever in ovens." And the other Rabbi says, "But, that won't hurt. I mean because if you are burning forever, you have passed the point where you dread it. It is eternal." And the other Rabbi, "I know, God will arrange so that they are always entering and always dreading the fire that will burn them." And still another Rabbi gathered around says, "Well, what about the Goyim, they didn't sign the covenant?" "Oh, but after Cain killed Abel, Adam was so disgusted that he left Eve for a thousand years and shacked up with Lilith again and the Goyim are wet-dream children." They evaporate. They don't suffer at all. This is a great universalizing masterpiece written in the same century as Dante's *Divine Comedy*. As far as I can see, those are the two great works at all of the imagination in the thirteenth century. Among the Hasidic doctrines there is a picture. God always tries to find a hammer and then the Jews pray that he won't renege before the hammer has exterminated all the Jews who have broken some part of the law. But he always breaks down before the work is done and consequently they have to go through it again. So by the Hasidic period, and parallel to Blake, by the way, and throughout Europe where this great, great visionizing goes on in Christian and again in Islam and in the Jewish world, what the Jews see is that there must be a holocaust and that they must pray that God [will] not suddenly become unable to endure the suffering of the holocaust so that he will finish the job of killing. This picture as it goes out in our century where the ones that belong to the covenant were breaking the literal covenant and God does not intend the covenant to be a metaphor. This holocaust left huge communities who break the law. So, it failed again.

[Question from the audience about the nature of Judaism]

That is one thing that Hillman sees is that the divine has its character. Certainly we can't pose a Christos who, as Hillman can see, who is a God of love. And if you go to the New Testament, you find the barest thing that the Christos does is announce that the father will be love. The one that the Old Testament announces he is wrath, jealousy. It is a full scoreboard as in

the Greek world. My trouble with Hillman is that he won't see
that the Greek world is also the divine and also has this character.
Yet he does see it. He says that we have to pay attention to the
shadow. But I am not talking about, are Jews, Jews? In this sense.
I am alarmed by the idea that there is a race. There is a breed perhaps, but anthropologically, it is un-understandable that there is a
race. Only the Germans and the Jews agreed. In a century in
which anthropologists have come to see, no, this isn't a race at all,
this is a group of people, like the Pythagoreans, who didn't in-
termarry. Originally in the Old Testament the Jews married outside their tribe. But I am not talking about Judaism. I was talking
about these works from the Jewish experience of the divine
where we see how much they are like the things we know about
Christianity. Yes, I know, the poet Carl Rakosi felt that Rothenberg should never have published his *Big Jewish Book*, and I said,
"You mean that you don't want the world to know that the Jews
are like we are? You want the Jews to be a rational people when
no one else is?"[42] Would you vote that the Americans are rational, running across the continent killing the Indians left and
right, burning the forests back for their own real estate? What I
was talking about was the experience when you were in this state
what you begin to know. Not like when you come out of it. We
aren't always in that state. The body finds it painful coming to
that state and the soul goes with it so that soul doesn't love that
state. As a matter of fact, I said enrapture and so forth is very
much like being raped. This thing that mounts up and establishes
the threshold in which we come to the divine.

Let me read this passage. It is the occurrence of the eidolon. I
have waited for some time for it to appear and I had translated
the brief fragment from Pindar over and over and over again until
I have forgotten and only my hands felt. Pindar says in the pas-

---

[42] *A Big Jewish Book: Poems & Other Visions of the Jews from Tribal Times to the Present,* ed. Jerome Rothenberg with Harris Lenowitz and Charles Doria (Garden City,
NJ: Anchor Press/Doubleday, 1978). Carl Rakosi (1903-) is one of the original
"Objectivist Poets." His *Selected Poems* (New York: New Directions, 1941) was an
important early book, while *Collected Poems* (Orono, ME: National Poetry Foundation, 1986) presents a summary of his writing. Rakosi lives in San Francisco and was a
friend of Robert Duncan's.

sage that he saw the eidolon in a dream and a friend, Norman Austin, who wrote a marvelous book *Archery at the Dark of the Moon*, wrote and said that he was sending me that book.[43] And I thought, "My God, I know a Greek scholar when I meet one," but he wrote: "The eidolon came to me in a dream and I found him in Pindar." Try that on for size to come along with a book supposedly about Homer.

THE RECITAL OF THE PINDAR: [fragment 131 (96)]
   July 7-8 1979

Companion,   hold steady the beat of the fire that burns me out.

Yet another body—it is like an everlasting flow of tears, a river I am of, passing, the watery weave of the bond itself and its bounda- ries—where was I bound?— in the fullness of its time remains. The Elohim work their figure of me in the fire storm cloud.   There is something in me that terrifies me,   something   beyond me.   In the savage intent   he sleeps where I wake,   his strength lies entranced where I move   and we two would embrace to touch and release our human bond in his bind.

Deep we go down to die   in the beast by the stream where the flow of tears has never ceased   we thirst and would perish,   the human yearning blossoming up, beautiful bud and full flower, from the stem of remorseless hunger.   Do not see that my glare would be toucht by your seeing me again?   And yet, when we sleep,   this fierceness re- turns before us, waking   in dream and in the spell of speech   the trance of deep poetry his roar   the water roaring   lion - rose - flame rising round   as the flood rises.[44]

Now for some forty years I had been seeing over and over again that those figures of the eidolon as the lion-headed figure with

[43] Norman Austin, *Archery at the Dark of the Moon: Poetic Problems in Homer's Odys- sey* (Berkeley: University of California Press, 1975).
[44] This passge is the final section of "Eidolon of the Aion," in *Ground Work I: Before the War*, 158. Italics appear in the text as published.

those snakes around our rivers [were] in this. But it came forward in poetry. You prepare to see the image by searching for it. You don't find it by searching for it at all. You prepare to see it when something much more mysterious than the searching happens. Something that is not searching when in a sense you are not looking for it. You are waiting. The search is exhausting. The search, is as a matter of fact, isn't finished by having an appearance. This immediacy does not end the search. But the presentation becomes and is immediate. And you have long prepared to recognize it. And Robert Graves, who says in a point, it is not important that a god appear, what is important is that you recognize that you are actually looking at the god. Since we all know that a god appears. And that is the way gods love to slip into the picture—I just had a divine evening. It must come from something else and it comes from a conjunction in the poem. Let's go to "Alchemical Blue" and read some of it. I am going to read at least opening passages.[45] In Hillman's own mind, I am sure he thinks that he is writing a kind of vast resource for the lore of the metals or minerals.

Alchemical Blue and the Unio Mentalis

the soul
vanishes
the soul. vanishes.   into the
shape of things.
—Robert Kelly, "The Blue"

TRANSITIONS FROM BLACK TO WHITE sometimes go through a series of other colors, notably darker blues, the blues of bruises, sobriety, puritan self-examination; the blues of slow jazz. Silver's color was not only white, but also blue. Ruland lists 27 kinds of blue-colored silver. Norton writes: "Silver may easily be converted into the colour of the lazulite, because. . . silver, produced by air, has a tendency to become assimilated to the color of the sky." So strong is the association of blue with silver and whitening, that even when modern chemistry dis-

---

[45] James Hillman, "Alchemical Blue and the Unio Mentalis," *Sulfur*, no. 1 (1981): 33-49. Duncan does not read Hillman's notes for the text on page 33, and at the end of his lecture on page 34.

putes alchemical testimony (deriving a blue pigment from silver treated with salt, vinegar, etc.), it assumes the alchemists had some to-us-unknown physical justification for their claim. Is not the claim based rather on fantasy, a sophic silver of a whitened imagination which *knows* that blue belongs to silvering, and therefore *sees* it?

Not until you have the claim based rather on fantasy do you have any appearance at all of what saturates most of Hillman's writing which is: I am preaching the doctrine of fantasy. I am going to tell you why this is seen now, but we have absolute evocation of blue and silver and so forth. And more than that, the statements, although the footnotes may substantiate them, actually exist far beyond the mere event. They are no longer nervous for the fact. To go back to another passage of Keats that Hillman could have also read with great care was the idea of existing in uncertainties, doubts and so forth as creative source.[46] There is no moment in which you can say what the thing is. You can't say it is fantasy, so if you get with fantasy, it will occur, because it has already occurred in here. It is absolutely coming forward. He can't say this is research. That is the other kind of statement and it is all around. Even that wonderful turn is not "the claim based rather on fantasy, but a sophic silver of a whitened imagination." That again is right into the poet's hands saying that you have got to think by fantasy. It is absolute imagination that tells him the true nature of fantasy is a sophic silver of the whitened imagination which knows that blue belongs to silvering and therefore sees it. Sees is in italics, knows is in italics and we have already begun to see we are not knowing things where there is no psychoanalytic doctrine. And we are in the presence of things that the imagination is immediate to and is telling us for the first time, as far as I know, that fantasy is now not a perspective, but is itself a mineral, "a sophic silver of whitened imagination." And these are things that the imagination knows indeed about the mineral world.

---

[46] "—I mean *Negative Capability*, that is when man is capable of being in uncertainty, Mysteries, doubts, without any irritable reaching after fact and reason—" Letter of John Keats to George and Thomas Keats, 22 December 1817.

> The blue transit between black and white is like that sadness
> which emerges from despair as it proceeds toward reflection.
> Reflection here comes from or takes one into a blue distance,
> less a concentrated act that we do than something insinuating it-
> self upon us as a cold, isolating inhibition.

So an inhibition also belongs to the mineral world. It is also
seen, felt, a thing. The word "something" is absolute there. "This
vertical withdrawal is also like an emptying out, the creation of a
negative capability." That was the one I said he could have looked
at in the course of writing *Re-Visioning Psychology*. He certainly
had been into and back and forth; he evoked Keats. "The creation
of a negative capability, or a profound—listening already an inti-
mation of silver. Well, it is proceeded by "Silver and White
Earth," *Spring*, (1980).[47] So it is an ongoing business. When he
went into this flow of absolute knowledge about the nature of the
world, we have jazz come in. Not only does my reading follow a
line I feel of an absolute music and this is a jazzy passage, but he
evoked jazz itself. So jazz is present. The blue of jazz, not "the I
feel blue," haunts Hillman. One of his real subjects isn't depression, it is something more than—isn't it a need of the soul? The
soul that creates depression, doesn't enter it, and so forth, but
creates it. In the religion of my family, things were like depres-
sions were thought of and we were taught as children by having
chrysalises and seeing moths emerge from them and seeing the
change of worm into the moth that incubation was what a depression was. And we didn't picture nothing going on inside this
chrysalis. The body is changing, but the spirit is changing, the
soul is changing and that is a long suffered depression. The world
is not there, it looks inert. It has wrapped itself up. That is not
metaphor about something that happens to human beings. The
insect tells us what incubation is because we can see it and now
we recognize that we are also a chrysalis. That we are also the
psyche/butterfly. And in this light, Psyche, the butterfly, was not

---

[47] "Alchemical Blue and the Unio Mentalis" is a chapter from a long study "Silver
and the White Earth," the first part of which appeared in *Spring: An Annual of Archetypal Psychology and Jungian Thought* (1980): 21-48.

thought of as the soul, by the way. Not in the hermeticism of my family. For them the soul was the one you find in Homer, the shade. They called that up to their seance tables. And they knew that it could arrive and chatter and chitter and be insubstantial and would draw from everything around in order to achieve even voice.

These very experiences Goethe associates with blue:

> ...blue still brings a principle of darkness with it...As a hue it is powerful, but is on the negative side, and its highest purity is, as it were, a stimulating negation...a kind of contradiction between excitement and repose.

> As the upper sky and mountains appear blue, so a blue surface seems to recede from us.

> ...it draws us after it.

> Blue gives us an impression of cold, and thus, again, reminds us of shade. We have before spoken of its affinity with black.

> Rooms which are hung with pure blue, appear in some degree larger, but at the same time empty and cold.

> ...objects seen through a blue glass are gloomy and melancholy.

Well at last Hillman at this place has become a peer of the poet Goethe. Certainly for early years in psychoanalysis, there is a great superstition about the creative personality. Seeing the poets, the musicians, that really had some divine contact—as if the divine could possibly be closer to something than to everywhere—than the analyst had. And lots of fantasies about are we to release the creativity of the patient and then the feeling that all science takes a vow: I am not being creative, I am not being creative, I am not being creative. This is the real stuff. Occultists always had this, by the way. The one thing that is intolerable to occultists is that they might be making it up. Now this is evoking the entrance. I don't think he created it, he was trained for it in *Re-*

Visioning Psychology. That was Goethe's voice; it is exactly the
same voice as the part we call Hillman's, because we have
emerged in that other poetry that Rilke talked about in which all
poets are the servitors and servants of the existence of a realm
called poetry and of a poem. So the shift from Hillman to Goethe
is the shift from an absolute fellow mind. It belongs where it is.
The critics are still talking about how interesting and are still
quoting passages from other people. But in this domain where it
is the poetic voice, the voice is the voice of all events in poetry, so
it can speak again where it has always spoken. Here I find exactly
that. So, what is he doing when he says these very experiences
Goethe associates with blue? Hillman and Goethe: are they both
psychoanalysts, are they both poets? What is it that these very
experiences are present to?

> Sadness is not the whole of it. A turbulent dissolution of the ni-
> gredo can also show us as blue movies, blue language, *l'amour
> bleu*, blue beard, blue murder, and cyanotic body. When these
> sorts of pornographic, perverse, ghastly, or vicious an-
> ima/animus fantasies start up, we can place them within the
> blue transition toward the albedo. Then we will look for bits of
> silver in the violence. There are patterns of self-recognition
> forming by means of horror and obscenity. The soul, putrefac-
> tion is generating a new anima-consciousness. A new psychic
> grounding that must include underground experience of the an-
> ima, itself, her deathly and perverse affinities.

So now the anima belongs to the creative realm. She is being
made up. She is not our factor of creativity. In that passage I
started about Hillman's trouble about the humane and human,
that belongs to the purely creative. Hillman's complaint is that
we are no longer with Pandora's box of gifts. Actually the human
and the humane is a pure creation, consequently, like psyche, is
ephemeral. It only takes place to the degree and where we create
it and we can't inherit it or be given it as a gift at all. Both Adams
and Jefferson saw that the trouble with the Bill of Rights is Rights
are things you create and need, nothing that the law can give you.
If it is given, you don't need it. Period. If it is given, you don't
even come up to anything you need at all. The Bill of Rights is

experienced only when you haven't got them and then you actually fight and are willing to die for them. But if it is given for you, there is no claim, and they produce the opposite effect, which is lawful inertia in all the realms of essential rights. So Jefferson and Adams writing back and forth: Adams said is it because we are lawyers that we wrote it into a law? Both of them having a horror of what law is.[48] Which is a contract instead of a living experience that you actually fight for. The minute you actually have to have a right, by the way, you will find out the Bill of Rights won't give you nothing and you are in there fighting tooth and nail. And you can't justify a right by the way. A right is not from justice, it is from need. The same one that Eros is from. By the time you're rationalizing it, writing out a covenant where you will have it, you're not in the actual violent creativity of right coming into existence.

Let me close, then, with the going on from the anima trends.

> There are patterns of self-recognition forming by means of horror and obscenity. The soul's putrefaction is generating a new anima consciousness, a new psychic grounding that must include underworld experiences of the anima itself: her deathly and perverse affinities. The dark blue of the Madonna's robe bears many shadows, and these give her depths of understanding, just as the mind made on the moon has lived with Lilith so that its thought can never be naive, never cease to strike deep toward shadows. Blue protects white from innocence. [49]

---

[48] *The Adams-Jefferson Letters; The Complete Correspondence between Thomas Jefferson and Abigail and John Adams,* ed. Lester J. Cappon, 2. vols. (Chapel Hill: University of North Carolina Press, 1959).

[49] *Sulfur* no. 1: 33-34.

WIND AND SEA, FIRE AND NIGHT

ROBERT DUNCAN

This is a transcription of a lecture given by Robert Duncan at a conference entitled "Anima, Animal, Animation," in Buffalo, New York, 23 November 1980, sponsored by the Analytical Psychology Society of Western New York. The transcription attempts to represent the flow of Duncan's thought; in like manner, the punctuation attempts to translate the lecture from an oral presentation to a printed text. Duncan's mind worked very quickly, often with multiple frames of reference operating at the same time. Like anyone lecturing without a prepared text to read from, Duncan started sentences, dropped them, and began again. Some of these have been deleted. He also had the habit of combining vastly different ideas in the same sentence, and also in long runs of monolog. I have attempted to transcribe these as close to the oral text as possible. At times it was necessary to insert words to make the sense hold as a text for reading. These insertions appear in square brackets. Notes have been added as a way of clarifying allusions and references in the text. The lecture was transcribed and edited by Robert J. Bertholf. Printed with the permission of the Literary Estate of Robert Duncan. © The Literary Estate of Robert Duncan.

THOMAS KAPACINSKAS[1]: *"Paul Kugler told me long ago that poetry actually happens in some way in Buffalo, that people actually turn out for poetry readings like they do for football games elsewhere, and I was stunned actually. I don't know what your response to the evening [poetry reading by Robert Duncan] was, but for me it was truly memorable. I'm going to read this little bit of information because that's what one is supposed to do:*

"Robert Duncan was born in Oakland, California in 1919. He lived in New York during World War II. He edited The Experimental Review *there. He says that in the early 1950s his work appeared in* Origin, *later in* The Black Mountain Review *edited by Robert Creeley. He has lived on the West Coast these many years as part of the famous San Francisco 'Renaissance.' And now he teaches poetics in the New College in the City of San Francisco in a program that I believe is devoted to the history and philosophy of ideas. He's a person of genius: Robert Duncan."*

This should suggest I'm going to be impulsive, which is quite true. It isn't that hard to run into fire, water, night, and wind in my work. Pat[ricia Berry] is the one that gave that wonderful description of what you do, and you also reach for generously wide titles, but "Anima, Animal, Animation" is the thing.[2] Since I have a sort of poetic zoo, there would be an effect for me of tending those damn animals all over again. I have a feeling of the universe itself—pardon me Aristotle—as having birth and death, that is, going from birth to death. And I certainly do, but there everybody will cooperate. I mean, our contemporary sciences also have a picture of the universe, don't they, that's alive. It goes from birth to death. Whatever principle that life is. The whole proposition of animation or of anima was the one that I went back to with fire, wind and what is the unnamable one? But what I found curious in our series was night. I real-

---

[1] The introduction is by Thomas Kapacinskas, President of the Chicago Jung Institute.

[2] Patricia Berry is the author of *Echo's Subtle Body: Contributions to an Archetypal Psychology* (Spring Publications, Dallas, 1982) and edited *Fathers and Mothers: Five Papers on the Archetypal Backgrounds of Family Psychology* (Zürich, Switzerland: Spring Publications, 1973).

ize that, as I turned away from the phone, that night seemed to be inanimate to me. Night appears as a nurse in my work—water was the other one, wasn't it?[3] Wind, water, and fire have been proposed since the earliest times as to what it would be that would make us alive. A body has fire in it and the difference, for instance—that didn't need some other kind of medicine to notice that we only have to differ not many degrees in heat and it looks like that's what it is that makes you alive or not alive. And certainly we're very familiar with the test. We all run right away, "Is it still breathing?" That's what wind, however, we find that was not that much on our minds in the early one because we find that the whole idea of the conception of things, the wind moving across a water and that's the underlying nature of the life of earth or the life of universe. So that there will be waters under it, water in which its life comes. And winds all the time from which its life comes. And the winds we experience are reminders of *the* wind.

Certainly in my later work, and I think already in *Bending the Bow* there's a transformation of terms.[4] Our poetic tradition accents and looks to some people remarkably like Neo-Platonism and so forth, because we have not just the wind we saw outside today or a wind has come up but we have *the* wind that these others seem to be the actors of and that's in a stage that does look as if there was a divine wind. If not in *Bending the Bow*—it's lucky I don't have to pass an examination in yours truly—certainly later, I begin to find that I have to put certain terms like heaven in quotes, a little like Henry James has to put "chair" in quotes because it's in a curious character in his mind. It's still there, not moved at all, but it now must mean something quite different than you took it to mean in that first place. There are people who feel that every time science reproposes the universe all the other propositions must be passé, but in a poet's mind they're not passé at all or the sun wouldn't be rising and setting. That's so powerful, in my poetry. In guilty moments I have read criticism pointing out that we're really retrograde. I mean the news has been in

---

[3] See "Four Songs the Night Nurse Sang," in *Roots and Branches* (New York: New Directions, 1964), 59-63.

[4] Robert Duncan, *Bending the Bow* (New York, New Directions, 1968).

for a long time that the sun doesn't rise and—"Ah, I rose with the sun and we'll put it to bed." Those French poets wouldn't be able to move around in poetry. "Go to bed with me" is nothing in comparison with the whole, what's that one, going to bed at the end of the day. So that we keep alive, and I know that we gather many retrograde readers and we can soon have a whole moral majority because we're still doing with the sun what it says in the Bible. But that's not what's happening in the poem. What's happening in the poem is it won't give anything up that's ever moved in the language. We're harder headed than any fundamentalists ever would be because we're multiple, multiple, multiple, multiple fundamentalists. Meet your friendly fundamentalists and while they have an imaginary liberalism, and when they wake up to the fact that the fundamentalist next to them is sitting on a different fundament, they start hitting each other with much more vigor and deadliness than they'd ever bother with the people who sit and think they're in something else—liberals who have an argument about whether there's a fundament there or not. And so we ransack all psychoanalysis. Why? Because it raises new pictures. It's impossible insofar as we're poets to get us into line. It's just remarkable you can go to religious poets and you'll find that in the poetry things are behaving in a very different way. There are other areas of our feelings. If I have something that I believe, I think it's just the straight line of what I've read in *Scientific American* which changes faster than I do, so that's great, and no wonder I like that ground for my weekly belief. The belief of the week is about where civilization is.

Now, if you think about in the beginning and I in my beginning certainly, I don't know what they were doing—some of you are much younger and I know they straightened it out later—but as a child things like wind, water, well earth. I've certainly overconvinced that the entire physics was earth, air, fire, and water. That would do the whole trip. I expect to find earth in Mars and earth in Saturn and then it didn't bother me that earth would turn out to be something quite different. But wasn't water in the first place fire? In Theosophy wasn't man in the first place a dinosaur? Oh I love that because at ten I loved dinosaurs. Madame Blavatsky could have had me in her arms it began to dawn on you,[5] those people, in this place that's called Mu or something, those men are great reptile-shapes, and more than that they don't fit their shapes, they actually flow all over the place.[6] In childhood it was disappointing you got to the museum and the dinosaur—you can't really focus on it—it is much bigger than you are, but in your mind the dragon dinosaur went everywhere, every dinosaur or dragon you could meet looked dinky when you got there. It was a cross between is this all it is, oh wow, is this all it is, is about the right pitch for it?

And so that's another reason that water and fire and wind and night are tremendums for me. They're elements. In a Bunsen burner you're actually looking at fire and you could write down and you could get into your head what was happening there. That just expands. Every step you'd make most people would think would be reductive. In a company of Jungians we hear about reduction and the rest of us say, "How about reduction upward?" Reductions for a poet are not closures like this, reductions just make the big thing more monstrous. Try to reduce it. Logical positivism, for instance, I love, because by the time they get through, the poets own the whole universe. An earnest logical positivism shows us that there's no statement you can make. That's what the whole thing's about, so that every statement you must make must be pure poetry and the rest of the people being cautious are out of their minds. I mean the ones who think, "Halfway No" or, "A little, Yes, please." It just won't work. You've had enough sample of me to know what a sea's gonna look like. But this is a poem that amuses me because one of the strongest drives, and it came from a poet who is one of my masters, William Carlos Williams. You heard me talk about the tree but, when you hear somebody talking about having that, that tree out there, you must realize out there is difficult for me because I've just swallowed it. I have no trouble with Descartes because I

---

[5] Helena Blavatsky, (1831-1891) an influential Theosophist and author of *Isis Unveiled: A Master-Key to the Mysteries of Ancient and Modern Sceince and Theology*, 2. vols (New York: J.W. Bounton, 1877). See also Sylvia Cranston, (New York: G.P. Putnam's Sons, 1993). *HPB: The Extraordinary Life of Helena Blavatsky, Founder of the Modern Theosophical Movement.*

[6] Mu is another name for the lost continent of Atlantis.

ate it all up and didn't understand it at all. It's inside me. I establish an inside and an outside, and if I do that OK, that's fine. I still
haven't come to the other part of the tremendum, of what is the
enormous, of expansion, tremendum. I experience boundaries
and they're created too.[7]

All right, in *Heavenly City Earthly City*.[8] Here I lived in San
Francisco, it is my spiritual environment and I thought everything will be saved if I can just get this city in the sense that I see.
I wasn't going to imitate *Paterson* at all. The proposition was
coming forward to get that city the way it is, not realism, but I
understood that a spiritual city is intensified in its actuality, intensified when that expansion can, intensify, can come down to
focal points. Well, and that city is on the Pacific. What I want to
read because its part of the water, but it will be water and fire
right away and certainly animals. I knew it was gonna be animals
no matter what passage I know, would read. This was my attempt
at realism. By the time I'm here, I realize I've flunked realism but
I'm in something else. One thing you can't do in a poem is start,
"Please can I have another chance. I'll take the course again and
keep my mind on it." You just can't do that. And you actually
arrive by flunking out of something, of, maybe part of the as-
signment. I hope I'm not covering for the possible flunk out of
talking about earth, water. OK. And this is just the Pacific, just
off our shores. It should have its rocks. I know how to do it, and
you go out, get the names and get the contours or whatever.

The praise of the sun is a didactic poem.

That even promises that it's gonna [be] instructive and will be
with what it looks like off our shores.

The ape and his raiment of gold or cloth of fire

---

7 Rudolf Otto, *The Idea of the Holy: An Inquiry Into the Non-rational Factor in the
Idea of the Divine and Its Relation to the Rational*, trans. John W. Harvey
(Oxford: Oxford University Press, 1923). Duncan is drawing on Otto's discussion of "Tremendum," and later in this lecture refers to the "Numen" which is
also discussed by Otto.
8 Robert Duncan, *Heavenly City Earthly City* (Berkeley: Bern Porter, 1947).

apes the categories of the spiritual man
and, in the teaching, learns from his raiments
the torturous lessons of his apish form.
What man knows more than his cloth of gold
who fixes his eye upon his source? I know no more
than the fleshly life that clothes in its ardor
the bony rigor of my inward form.
The lineaments of my body are
a didactic poem,
the apish chiaroscuro of my source, the sun.

And now I'll read the place where the ocean comes in.

The praise of the sun is a nostalgic poem.
The tum-tum-tum in memory
is like the pounding surf in dreams.
The man in the solitude of his poetic form
finds his self-consciousness defined
by the boundaries of a non-committal sea
that washes, washes the reluctant mind,
and carves its shores its secret coves.

Sometimes our feelings are so mild
they are like a day when rocks
seem mere extensions of the sea
washt in a world of oceanic blue
and continents seem dreams of a watery deep.

Turbulent Pacific! the sea-lions bark
in ghostly conversations and sun themselves
upon the sea-conditioned rocks.
Insistent questioner of our shores!
Somnambulist! old comforter!
You wright in passion's storm and passionate calm
your reasonless change and see to restore
the aspiring man to your green remote.

The individual ape in the human sea

is worn, is worn by a non-committal tide,
and shows in his unnecessary watching face
the necessary convolutions of that sea,
the memories of forsaken lands.

The praise of the sun is a nostalgic poem;
sometimes the sea seems mild and light
as a luminous harp upon which the sun plays
threaded with indolent wires of gold
across the ruddy music of its waves
and its voices merge in a pulsing counterpoint
to sing the wonders of the sun,
the beasts of the sun and the watery beasts.

Sea leopards cough in the halls of our sleep,
swim in the wastes of salt and wrack of ships,
and sun themselves upon the resounding rocks,
or lie in the thoughtless shallows of the sun.
These are the tides of the poetic sea.
I drift, I drift. The praise of the sun
is purposeless. I dream of those forsaken shores
wrapt in the mind's redeeming haze.
Sea leopards cough in the halls of our sleep;
disturb the course of the nostalgic sea,
casual hints where harmlessly they swim
of some brooding fear in the fiery deep.

The earth has tides of desolation and of bliss,
of shadows and of amber marbled surfaces,
laments and cries, vague intimations of the sun,
terrors, brightnesses of noon, and groves
of memory: in these her beauty is renewd.
The wandering man returns to his city
as if he might return to earth a light, a joy,
and find his rest in earthly company.

The praise of the sun is a renewing poem.
The earth replenishes, replenishes her beauty

and sings a green praise of her terrible source.
The sea reflects, reflects in her evening tides
upon some lavender recall of some past glory,
some dazzle of a noon magnificence.
The evening hour is eloquent of the sun.
This is no dominion of the pure terror
but soothes, soothes. We walk in the light
of beauty's calm. Our city lies about us
murmuring, drifts in an evening humanity.

There is a wisdom of night and day,
older than that proud blaze of the sun,
in which we rest, a passion, primitive to love,
of perishing, a praise and recreation of the sun.
My earthly city is reveald in its beauty.[9]

Poetry has many fierce groups with many ideas of what the poem
is. My own poetry from its earliest stages, or my own mind and
my own world, belongs to that tradition in which we inhabit a
creation and are creatures. The news is leaking through that that's
not universal. If we were to try to find universals this would not
work. That is profoundly a creation and we were profoundly
creatures excludes me from the happy Buddhism in which the
work you're on is all an illusion. It's just impossible. I have no
such sense of it. Intellectually it's very inviting. The mind interestingly can actually and very boldly, under pain under anything
it wants, demote us from everything and decide its an illusion.
But poetry comes with too many signals. Whalen at one point
said I don't see why you're not a Buddhist.[10] I said, "Yes," but I
don't just write with my brain. It isn't excluded and it would like
to hold many other things in contempt, but I write with my
hands and you just announced that my hands are an illusion and

---

[9] *Ibid*. 29, 31-33.

[10] Philip Whalen (1923-), American poet, who was part of the San Francisco
"Renaissance," and who, along with Lew Welch and Gary Snyder, enbraced
some branches of Buddhist thought. *On Bear's Head* (New York: Harcourt,
Brace & World, Inc., and Coyote, 1969) is a collected book of poems which
demonstrates Whalen's affiliations with Buddhism.

my hands happen to have a lot of authority in this funny little democracy I run. They, when they're offended, can really make trouble so I will just stay with this creature, creation, and so forth. Hands of course want to think of it as a creation. Who is it that's speaking when it's all a creation? The only pictures we've got of what man knew when he built a vase, so the first was playing paddy-cakes and making a little man out of dough. It's all hands and the next one is the marvelous discovery, that's it's woven, another thing I think the hand knows a lot about. That's where the hand found out it's faster than the eye. When you do a piece of ceramics, oh my, the eye says, "Oh my, look at that," and the hands going like this, you know, and the feel, and the eyes say, "Oooooh I'm a creator look at this thing." But with this other one the eye can't listen—what's going on here? And the hand goes here. So I write with a pen and am amazed when the lines I write are in front of me. You can see why I was talking about inside and outside too. I'm talking about in front of my eyes. Me, no of course, that's the one where we'll go back and say what is the division, it's curious indeed that me is eyes when I'm looking, and this is me. When you have the sense my hands did it or my eyes, then you wonder who is it that's saying this. Who is it that's ruling now? If I have an ache, maybe it's my hip that has me, sort of things. It works in the poem because we're interested not, let's say not in the psychological and psychological question of who, but we need more than one me in there to do this business. So if we find ourselves here, we don't throw this one away, we bring in from anywhere, as a matter of fact, as fast as I answered on the telephone or as Pat's description and your impulse will be right because it's just that you have to start getting the whole thing going. And these I gave, water, fire, wind, and night were posed almost immediately as being the animators of the world that is before me when I'm writing. When they appear, they seem to be animating the life forces. There's a fire in the language, and I have only to summon it up, and I find myself actually getting the state you saw me in last night when I'm reading. I have to come to a language for that. But I use more than most people use of words that are telling you and me what's coming up. Many people have trouble with William Carlos Williams's poetry. There I can feel the fire, so when you see lots of key words, deep, and so forth, you know that I have to summon up those things to be in this state. The state is not more or less at all. Many readers when they turn to Williams don't find these key words about a promise of beat. They don't find him invoking death, fire, water, in this way. They feel there's no poetry there. There is something between the intonation of the part, which is both the melody and the immediate sound and its resonances that the poet recognizes, the poet recognizes, the poet recognizes. Often that's what's dismissed. People respond to that. People respond to such a rhythm but when they have an expectation, let's say of a particular rhythm they've heard, they'll fail to hear subtler ones. Certain periods, it seems to me, may develop very subtle rhythms when they have an audience that's following that and wanting more of it, and find themselves isolated. I remember in the period when we were intensely reading John Donne, it was amazing to discover that [Ben] Jonson said of Donne that he wouldn't be read for hundreds of years because he had gone into poetry with such a rhythm and a complexity that was so dependent upon the fact that that period had an audience that listened to the music of it that way. Jonson knew about you'd only have to lose the Tudor state, the state in which everyone enjoyed tremendous conflict attention and so forth within a composition. Right after that men are going to start cutting off the king's head as if they could get rid of that feeling between themselves, and would there be a king and they turned into two sides. That's our period, very much. We can't contain a series of propositions yet we still are containing them. Our poetry contains very strange orders, extreme radicalism and an absolute conservatism, so we can turn around and say of conservatism, moral majorities, with great scorn that they don't resemble what's in our mind at all. And the same with a whole other area.

The sea can often be the deeps. I suddenly speak of the shallows of the sea, and I think about depth psychology would be something more interesting than amusing to have some shallow psychology. We've heard a little silly shallow psychology here. Can't you see the sign that says shallow psychology, and they think maybe that's maybe half an hour, and they say, no half an hour's too deep. We're going to take fifteen years. It's a marvelous proposition, I also have a mercantile mind. Fifteen years and we'll spread out your two million dollars over that area and that's what we call shallow. It's sort of a warm ground in which things will grow. But that warm ground in which things grow and mix is very much what I come from. That's the sun and the water, you can see that the images are at the tideland. They're in the tidelands and heights are someplace back there where the mountains are and depths are over here. They're not there at times. You can see them because my poetry will immediately bring up those little key words, not very original, just deep—this is deep, this is high. We've got it just like in Chinese paintings: "Wow," that looks high, and then we've got the feel, then we can be with the painting and it might be very simple because we inhabit feel, feels, not yet fields, in a poem. Everything told me I should not have them, that's probably where I got the idea. One thing I did understand in poetry is that there are other places. Nos are real warnings, like, "No, you don't put your hand in the fire to get the experience of fire." In a poem you do put your hand in the fire to get the experience of fire. As far as I can understand when you're really into the poem proposition, that's the only place in which we have a lovely corner of needed irresponsibility, and actually not only is practical, but you're not going to have any disastrous results. Well there's some people who are sure that poems are causing trouble. By irresponsibility I began to over-construct, over-compose. And that's typical of schools. I mean they're dominated anyway by their engineering departments, their health departments, and so forth, and it did dawn on me all of a sudden, why am I constructing this poem as if it were a bridge? There are no trucks going to drive over it and if they drove over it they're not going to collapse into the something beneath. There's no such proposition, and in a period when engineering is our top thing, people were constructing paintings that way, wondering if it would fly apart if it didn't have all these girders that you see in structures to be sure it doesn't fly apart. There's no way it's going to come off that canvas, that's where it's taking place. I had a very intense sense of the area, the time in which a poem takes place and this is what helped to lift this.

Wondering if I can do here, but in a poem it's very difficult for me because I am the one who over-constructs. For sixteen years my whole head was gonna be architecture. So you can see I tend to architect all the way through when I'm doing a poem and I love big structures that I then dismiss or dissolve or move around, as you could not a building.[11] The two things I can hear throughout our society, and they must be psychic things if you hear two—first one is this business what is gonna happen with the poem if it isn't constructed? This is a character armor school of thought. I am a character armor, so I don't worry about it at all. We're back at insects, my beautiful carapace, and you'll want me to take it off? In order to be your Reichian picture.[12] Rolf me, but you'll never rolf my carapace and that's an important part. I mean, that's the real things, you just didn't observe all that stuff, we took millions of years of evolution to get that glossy, hard, shell thing you think is not me.

And the other one I hear is discipline. Oh, I mean now at last, we've come to a period of sexual permissiveness. In the 1930s when discipline came up I didn't know what to answer. They'd say that isn't discipline, it's the same picture, that bridge isn't discipline and I'd say well, discipline now is no longer rightly part of poetry courses, it's really in the S & M column of personals. While I realize that a lot of poetry is over there, they really ought to be in the S & M. I can see a filler at the bottom of the S & M column. The poem of the day. You put the little verse in there and there will be a well disciplined verse, and next to it will be a naughty verse that needs discipline. No wonder I wanna go to all elemental. It is actually inviting to the artist to construct water, or to construct wind, or to construct fire, or to construct night.

---

[11] See Duncan's poem "The Architecture: Passages 9," in *Bending the Bow*, 26-28. The poem "Often I Am Permitted to Return to a Meadow" contains the line "Wherefrom fall all architectures I am." *The Opening of the Field* (New York, Grove Press, 1960), 7.

[12] Wilhelm Reich (1897-1957) was a German psychologist/philosopher whose books, *The Function of Orgasm: Sex-economic Problems of Biological Energy*, trans. Theodore P. Wolfe (New York: Noonday Press, 1961), and *Selected Writings: An Introduction to Orgonomy* (New York: Straus and Giroux, 1973) influenced some parts of contemporary American poetry.

These are the departments. One of the strong figures I've gotten that fascinated me—it came in, it came in my first five or six years, I heard of a king Canute who ordered the sea.[13] We know one discipline that Yahweh comes down and parts the Red Sea, that's a submissive Red Sea was my reaction to that story, and it demoted the Red Sea, I mean, I thought, oh, put it off. Now that I know it's an entirely Semitic Arab affair, with Egypt on one side or something you might interfere with it. We need a new one where you part the Pacific, I mean we'll probably get it as they say, San Francisco deserves.

In the period of *Heavenly City Earthly City*, I'll venture I was not far into looking at, beyond the fact that you're keeping a general atmosphere of all the fabulous. Magic shape shifting, shape changing, transporting, transforming are all operations that are immediately telling in the poem. And in a well-behaved poem by the way, the one that has been in S & M discipline, we discover what the discipline is because it has device, terms and so forth. When we think about the S & M, the specificity of taking one area of the artist would work in the erotic and professionalizing it and restricting yourself to it, I think the same non-magic would occur. It would become more fascinating but the poem is not to become fascinating in that way. The poet likes to have a little touch of Medusa flash in and out, but it's got to use the fact that it could change into something else.[14] The lines are changing. It's just simple, you're working in an art in which you've got in time things that are very much there. But they're changing and there's a delight in their change. Particularly in language a change around lines of rhyme. Moon turns into June turns into soon. Its a line that can betray itself as it goes along, and it's one that almost in speech you want to curb in your child. They arrive at words they

---

13 In "The Venice Poem," Duncan wrote:
    Like Canute he plays sovereign to the sea.
    He sits for hours as if he might hold it back.
    eyes fixt upon the tide,
    cross-eyed king of one thousand lines.
Robert Duncan, *The First Decade: Selected Poems 1940-1950* (London: Fulcrum Press, 1968), 93.
14 Medusa, the Gorgon whose head Perseus cuts off.

shouldn't arrive at by just rhyming. If there's no meaning, words produce a tremendous effect on the adults around. As a child you discovered that a mere word you didn't know what it was could suddenly cause panic throughout the adult world around you. You'd just gotten it. You're playing it like a music. There's nothing when I evoke deep that would be the equivalent if I were going to do it seriously. There are poets that become actually infatuated with the fact that they can have this and we have some floating guru poets, into deep things and they will come out deep. I mean they all come out words as the poet goes. And then suddenly they say, "Gee, I can feel this, go back into this feeling, and I suddenly realize I'm a spiritual instructor out there." There is a kind of health in remembering you're working with words and you can then go further and further with those words as to what they do in all of us.

Those who've written little essays on my work maybe know all the answers, but I'm not clear whether how much or why I was into reading alchemical texts in that period. I would have been into reading things that were near it. My parents were Hermeticists and they went through a series of initiations and they had their texts so I read the texts.[15] The texts when I discovered they were in print, and I didn't have to graduate actually to find them different places and especially there were alchemical texts in print that had been in print all along, and translated into English. Thanks to A. E. Waite, for instance, you had tons of things to read.[16] And I read them and saw them as romances. They were

---

[15] The Hermetic tradition derives from Hermes Trismegistos, "thrice born Hermes," the Greek name for the Egyptian God Thoth. There are seventeen treatises in *Corpus Hermeticum*, texts dating from the first to the third century AD. These texts deal with a wide range of occult subjects from astrology to theology, and propound the idea of the unity of the universe in which all parts are interdependent. The dipolar laws of sympathy and antipathy hold all things in balance; but it is necessary for humans to experience rebirth through the vision of the whole universe.

[16] Arthur Edward Waite (1857-1942) was a member of the Golden Dawn Society and a very prolific writer and scholar on occult matters. Some of his principal books are: *The Book of Ceremonial Magic* (1898; reprinted, New York: Land's End Press, 1969); *The Real History of the Rosicrucians* (New York: J. W. Bouton,

very close indeed to fairy tales, and I'd always loved fairy tales. And they were sources of another kind. When you get to that, now the sea and the sun reappear in water and fire and in a romance. And often fairy tales you have the same, and we're really seeing over and over again a picture of a wedding of water and fire. Papa Freud made it so you saw it all around but so do fairy tales. At the blue bird level, they're careful that the water's in the pail. It is the water in the pail you're carrying and the fire on the hearth. It is the fire on the hearth, or in the match as you light something. It's those little ones that are all around us that are the moments, and those are the ones for instance that are present in William Carlos Williams. Now he doesn't have to say "deep." Isn't it interesting we say deep and that means that we feel the tremendum, yet the entire quality is there in the water in the pail, the entire quality is there in the fire. The child sees that. I was taught as a child to look into the fire. In fact, the Hermeticism of my parents, it comes out of Theosophy and out of the general folk religion, back of that, the whole. It existed in the Calvinist world, so there were both witches and Calvinists at the same time. Our counterpart of witches today are Communists, and our counterparts of the witch finders are the moral majority and those two show how tedious things get when you don't pay attention to the water in the pail. We get it in the tap, we turn it off and on. It's not off and on when it's in the pail. I can remember a world when the water was in the pail. That sounds like beyond the pale and into the pail. I mean maybe we gotta do a curious form here. But that's exactly how I had hoped things would occur. Rhyme tells that and suddenly do I not only have an idea here, but in a poem if that movement takes place, it doesn't cause a ripple of humor, I have to work with it. That's the way I proceed, and so I have less associations. Interestingly enough I'm permitted less associations but they all have to be ones that are appropriate to work or I'm in great trouble. A word like pail, the water's in the pail, since I am fascinated also by the idea of having a pail and being in and outside the pail, the minute beyond the

---

1888); *The Magical Writings of Thomas Vaughan* (London: Redway, 1888), and *The Holy Kabbalah* (New York: The Macmillan Co., 1929).

pale, the minute those two would even come together in my over-crowded brain but, now we're talking about the weaving, then, while I might be ingenious enough to do something, if it isn't telling already for me to work with, my ingenuity will only produce a conceit. And I'm not an artist of conceit. The amazing thing in the period of Shakespeare and of Donne is that [they] could work amazingly in conceits, and in our time the ones who work in conceits, like e.e. cummings, seem to come out trivial. I won't pursue this because a lot of this has to do with the stylishness of the conceits that we permit. I have the demand that we hate in large that, we need something to be deep. But I can turn around. The reason I know about water in the pail, a poet, Ian Hamilton Finlay, who is terrified by the vast.[17] And now a phobia, you think you run to your friendly analyst so you could live with a prospective line through horizons. He did what an artist does. He went and transformed a world so that if you look at a star you see the star in the pail. And the water's in the pail, and the pail it's not deep, the pail is, isn't ten inches deep, it's ten inches. Or as an artist he will manufacture a foot rule, and he's not worried. The foot rule is ten feet long and it transforms the horizon that it seems to measure into twelve inches. And there are transformations of this kind and the creativity is a thing you would think would insanely intensify, if you're afraid of large things, and they're brought in this way. The transformation has not made them dinky, it's not made them intense. A star reflected in a pail of water is a marvel, and you understand it in magician's magic what otherwise would [not be explained].

The lights of our city are in order for us not to encounter stars. Not bears, they're stuck in the zoo. Once the lights are all on and you try to look at a star you're not going to encounter space, you're not going to encounter your own area which used to be the marvel. We're running into night now. The most interesting thing to me about night, and it was when I was a child, was not just the night around me. I was taught another dream. The ones of you who are into the psychoanalytic view of dreams—it's in-

---

[17] Ian Hamilton Finlay (1925-) is a Scottish poet who has been one of the strongest advocates of concrete poetry. He established the Wild Hawthorne Press which has published most of his work.

teresting there are other ideas of dreams. I was taught to go to dreams to live there and if I came back, also it was explained to me [that] sometimes it's like returning home. You live in such and such address and you go to school and if you meet somebody you can tell them your address, 1200 Pearl Street. That isn't an address I never had since I was seven and a half years old and it isn't memorized. It means I went out and know where I'm going back, and I was taught the same thing about a dream. The place you're in when you wake up was more important. When you went into the dark and then you went back where you were. Now we go back to a story and the story tells us something else now. I spoke of this cult of psyche. This was a cult of dream land. I didn't go back to a psyche. As a matter of fact, I could go back very amusingly and find myself to be almost anything that was absolutely understood. Over there you will be in the second grade. You aren't in the second grade at home. Over there you will be a raven—that was absolutely understood. It went along with their being absolutely certain that you couldn't tell what you would be when you came back here after death. They had enough Buddhism like the Tibetans. Dead really is. I won't remember you know. You go to school and everybody around says don't remember your address, don't remember your address, don't remember your address, hoping you get somewhere. And that's going out into these elemental shapes. But in that business of going back, night meant to me a nurse. Daytime whatever dreams were thought of differently and as a matter of fact they do prove to be very interesting. Another dream in poet lore day, night, mare, and daydream or night dream and day dream or magic. They're two different kinds of dreams. I think this is called coming home to where you are. In the poem, think about it—you see me sailing out in the poem and I am always in a form. I was in one thing when I went from home to school. I can go but I must also remember that, and the poem is inscribed all the way through by my address, all the way through by these two places existing. Now we come close to what the art is. Not in order to come home, but you've advanced then to two different worlds you live in, home and school. The only reason there is an art is that there are two systems, two worlds, two things that actually seem to be beyond your being able to make a metaphor of one after another. Metaphor means bringing something there back to here now what does it look like. It don't mean thinking up something, there's no thinking up something by the way, about a metaphor. We have traditional metaphors but they're almost like maps of going there and coming back. But it's so specific that if you come home and discover you're a chipmunk at home, you are. Everybody would say that would be a metaphor. This is a metaphor of schoolboy at school. Charles Olson would be in a rage about metaphor, but metaphor means just that.[18] It means just that you bring what you assume is yourself but here you discover it's a chipmunk and there you discovered it was a schoolboy. I think the reason poetry has a way of touching is that actually everybody has this business of moving around. I'm certainly not fascinated by the idea, is there reincarnation after death? Because there are so many reincarnations between breakfast this morning and standing up here and doing this. What would be impressive about being a totally different something or others, I mean, would that be me if I weren't? What would I do with my body? That's why the quotes on "heaven." We can't get rid of heaven by sketching what the heavens are like. They will remain heavens. Isn't it interesting, what if we looked up and said the hells are up there and the heavens the other place down there and then we'd start digging and say, "Gee, it's awfully muddy down here in heaven, but we got *oil*! Oh heavens, we've got oil down there!" And then you've found out that it was exhaustible. Now we've got God as totally exhaustible. We still have some oil but we've got very little God we can draw on and put in the barrel like they used to. I mean people don't say these things. As I understand it, it doesn't even turn on the lights.

---

18 Charles Olson (1910-1970) was an American poet, author of the influential essay "Projective Verse" (1950) which provoked a literary movement known as "The New American Poetry." His celebrated work is a long poem, *The Maximus Poems*, ed. George F. Butterick (Berkeley: University of California Press, 1983). He was a friend and poetic ally of Duncan.

We'll let's go to fire.[19] I guess it does have to do with me. The first war that showed me that we were in for the real trouble—the real trouble is, I mean the one, the truth about the country. I'm American through and through and through and through, which means [I know] how profoundly *evil* and wicked we are. Even at school kids caught on that a lot of Indians have been killed and a country has been laid to waste, and right before our own eyes we saw our little daddies beaten down to the ground all in order to get their little bank accounts. We could tell that we were in a pretty bad place. Some of this comes out of the specific feelings of the Theosophical world. They're borrowing from the Hindu— our country had a karma—and my family, for instance, they'd look at the horoscope of the country and it looks bad. Don't worry. But I did understand from karma that you don't get punished for what you do, you *are* what you do. That's what I was taught on my mammy's knee. You are not punished by life, you are what you do regardless of what it is. So there is a work, and you work with what you do in art. I didn't see sewn into it that it was necessary you wouldn't come out worse as you were working with it, no matter what. They thought in terms of weaknesses and strength. They were all will to power people and even Hitler looked good for quite a considerable amount of the time; but our American will for power is of course clean compared with the others.[20] My reaction was a great extreme. I had too much power already. I mean I was exhausting my parents so I should've had the other extreme, which is to try a little to not have a little less will and a little less power, but maybe I was reading Lao-tse.[21] Could I possibly get down there? Even my weakness sounds a little over-strong. So you find me burning up the old place when we come to Korea. We're in that Korean war and

---

[19] In the following discussion, Duncan's idea about war and strife agree with those set out in his essay, "Man's Fulfillment in Order and Strife," in Robert Duncan, *Fictive Certainties* (New York: New Directions, 1985), 111-141.

[20] Duncan is referring to Nietzsche's book *The Will to Power*. See, for example, Friedrich Wilhelm Nietzsche (1844-1900) *The Will to Power*, trans. Walter Kaufmann and R. J. Hollingdale, ed. Walter Kaufmann (New York: Random House, 1967).

[21] Lao-tse (604-653) Chinese philosopher, the founder of Taoism.

it was the first one I [knew] absolutely. I mean my picture of the Second World War is you can only defeat Hitler at war by being more terrible than he is and then you'll be there. I mean there's only one way, he's working from terror, and if you go to war against that, even an underground war, you have to become more terrible. There's only terrorism. Finally the United States became considerably more terrible. Hitler at least was racist and he burned up the Jews. The United States would just burn up a whole city, I mean wipe it out regardless of who's there, and pick out targets because they weren't war targets and then they'd get the terror message. That's exactly what they did in the atom bombings and the bombing of Dresden. They picked out something that no one in Europe would believe would be a war target and showed, now they'll be scared. I understood that as a child. I was an infant terrorist and I'm still, as you can hear in the poems, I'm a terrorist. I had to learn I wanted to keep the things I had just burned up. I'm not sure that I experimented and found out that you don't have it to. I like the repeated *attack* with the thing still there.

Yes, I do remember that my family was haunted by Atlantis. No wonder water and sea is going to be there and the main thing was always its destruction. Their generation of Hermeticism thought the United States was the counterpart of Atlantis and it would discover something in physics that would be in the department of fire that would be the counterpart of the discovery that was in the department of water in Atlantis, and they would destroy the entire world. That's what I was raised in, and I was adopted by astrology and as an infant I understood I was of the last generation of Atlantis. Even this time I wouldn't come off it. I thought at first, "Wow, that was a great place, what a prized child. Tell me that story about Moses again, mommy." Moses's story wasn't the one of this Atlantis thing. I'm just talking about how much comes in. Now you can write a little case history. A lot of other goof-balls have had that and that doesn't result in a poem necessarily so there's gotta be another circuit for it. Williams Carlos Williams faces the Korean War. I was saying how the Second World War looked to me. I have anarchist friends who would gladly napalm your child if they were convinced it would be Hitler tomorrow. I mean they just wouldn't question about it. Yuk. And in relation to our wars, there they are as a species, they're into napalming and burning forests and they've always got a reason for it. I know it's not going to be cured because they think Communists are over there. There's many other "theys" who might think that good people are over there, bad people are over there, think of them. Protestants are over there, can you choose it? Oh yes, Jews are over there, or Arabs are over there or the Irish are over there. Oh My God, Irish over there! Oh! And they all come running out and they're back. It used to be shillelaghs and now it's machine guns. And I just say they're out of that old game. If you're looking at them like you looked at squirrels you'd say, "Oh well, the season." They're out and they gotta burn babies. Reasons don't signify. And William Carlos Williams was in some way getting it at that level. He called a book of stories in the middle of the Korean War, *Make Light of It*.[22] This book came out just as I'm in this poem, it's called "An Essay at War" and I was myself, of course, extremely angry. This level in which I've called my poetic insight, the war fascinates me. I see it then as revelation and there's something insulting about protesting knowing the truth. I could never get Americans in the Second World War to see that what they were doing was why they were always doing in some sense. I was thinking of Freud's answer to Einstein when he says, "But you don't realize that you're running this war all the time in order to have what you call a civilization, but you see them as policemen and you see them as permissions to do the things you think are so wicked over here."[23] You want to have a massive world organization, that's fine, except that, that world organization isn't doing it completely. If it were really doing it there it would also be doing it right here where that war is taking place too. And it would be

---

[22] William Carlos Williams, *Make Light of It: Collected Stories* (New York: Random House, 1950).
[23] See Sigmund Freud (1856-1939), *Civilization and Its Discontents*, tr. James Strachey (New York: W. W. Norton, 1961).

doing it as Hillman points out, inside.[24] There is no way not to do it completely if you were going to go into that battle and it is a battle. So, there is a picture. The war, by the way, is only one kind of strife so that what we're calling war is strife. You say because I'm in strife we're doing the killing but there are other reasons. Remember love is a reason, has always been our coarse excuse, love murders of whole families that were demented by passion. Passion is not only war but passion interests me as a reason you destroy cities. And aesthetics is! That's an ugly building—bang, boom, crash, burn. So there's plenty of room. Williams dedicated it to our troops in Korea. My efforts in relation to the war were not protests, but imagination of the war. Imagination of what's going on there and it is tremendum. It is our tremendum. We imagine that what we did in Vietnam. We aren't going to exploit it, my God, if you weren't going to exploit it, we wouldn't burn it down. At least in the days when you enslaved the peoples you only killed in small numbers because you wanted a lot of slave power. This strange rationalization area, but this *Make Light of It* and the theme coming forward in the poem was going toward "An Essay at War," trying to be at war was what I saw you had to do. It goes back to the karma thing. If I'm American, I am also at war because it's part of a total dream. We can't come to be world people only as Americans. There's no other way. We can't suddenly say, "Oh I have nothing American to preserve, I'm not American. And so I haven't got any of this stuff." I was protesting while that was going on. I think you see where in the dream sense, protesting is only one form of it and you got killed protesting. Protesting students did the same things that were going on in Vietnam. They started burning buildings. They had reasons, and we thought how alarming, gee students have gone ape. Forgetting that officially we had gone ape. We moved it over so we aren't seeing it, it was done over there but the same thing was taking place throughout the country.

---

[24] See James Hillman, *Re-Visioning Psychology* (New York: Harper & Row, Publishers, 1975) as well as the accompanying lecture by Duncan on Hillman in this volume.

You who have given your intellect to Love.

Now let's go back, the hearth fire, I start with the hearth fire of the Cro-Magnon, and then I came forth thinking about fire. It is the first named incarnation of Love. We burn with it. The fire of Hell. Pain. But it is also warmth. Demonic. But it is also light. The night is all about us. A darkness within which all known things exist. So, a moment before the appearance of one most feared or one most desired, or one most loved. Or. . . the centuries are all about us. A light to read by. Within us. A time within which all known things exist.

You who have given your intellect to Love
think of this light even as the light of Love.
Make Light of It, Williams says,
dedicating his volume of stories
"to our troops in Korea."   Let
even our troops in Hell who have
hell-fire return from their flame-throwers
thru flame to the fire that burns them.[25]

Pauline Kael[26] and I were in a movie, in an Eighth Street movie, at a film that the intelligentia go to and they showed a newsreel and here what they showed was a man running on fire and a group of men pouring flame-throwers on the man. Who was the man? He was a Jap soldier who had hidden in a cave, deserted from his army and hidden in a cave, and who were the men? They were Americans. Pauline and I were aghast because we were the only ones and we began to feel, will they see us, do they know? Everyone was clapping and cheering, "Wow, wow, hurray, hurray." In San Francisco a couple of middle age drunks

[25] Robert Duncan, "An Essay At War," *A Book of Resemblances: Poems 1950-1953* (New Haven, CT: Henry Wenning, 1966), 25-26.
[26] Pauline Kael (1919-) was a movie reviewer for *The New Yorker*. She is a prolific writer whose books include, *I Lost It at the Movies* (Boston: Little, Brown, 1965) and *Movie Love: Complete Reviews 1988-1991* (New York: Dutton, 1991). She and Duncan were students together at Berkeley in 1938, and remained friends throughout Duncan's life.

come stumbling out of a bar, the woman is Irish, and the man is a Jap. He falls, and suddenly the crowd starts kicking him. There are three of us but we stand around. We protest, we don't know how to enter this scene at all. So that things like this are coming right into the poem. There are places where life initiates you and if you carry those, they're as specific as they used to be in the Greek mysteries. We discovered that, yes, we'll really cut your hand off and you can do the Zen thing. No this really happens here. Did they really eat someone in that scene? I think we are in a series now in religion where there's a transformation from eating someone, but we're not only talking now about, that in psychotic states they do it, but think about the place where they actually undergo, and that became part of the language. In a way the term is called a shadow. Let it mean everything it means in the Jungian thing, but the shadow means many, many things, but this is a shadow cast in which we read something that's gone. I'm thinking now let's say the shadow on the wall when everything else is gone—that was so remarkable to everybody when the atom bomb exploded and the one place where—no, man, you can't even find it but the shadow's there burned into the wall. These words or these things appear like that because they do have marks of events that you can find. In the art that's almost a level of which they're true to even what goes on in here. The reason they're so resistant—I'm suddenly attending them with a great deal of focus—is because they're very much there and I keep the sharpness of that shadow. If I can convey this I'm not thinking about will I psychoanalyze this thing. Well, but, I wanted to give how much there were things or experiences that don't, the imagination can thoroughly do this. One of the places you would suspect it is when there's a great deal of care and it looks like I'm becoming less associative in the passage, as if I'm being very careful.

It is Love. It is a hearth.
It is a lantern...

That's just after hell fire returns from their flame-throwers, through flame to the fire that burns them. Remember in every

circle of hell usually we think there are just sinners there but the
devils are there and they can't move around either. The flame-
throwers and the person in flames are in hell. It took some time
to realize that they're the ones who are confined. In Dante's Hell,
all sin means is that you can't move, that you won't let it go,
which he's instructed, until you find out it's not a punishment,
it's what they don't let go. And at first you think those sinners
aren't letting it go, but the flame-throwers aren't letting it go either. "Oh god, it's so boring here. All over again we gotta get our
kicks out of this." And the screams are the same. Oh Lord, I
mean I wish they would faint once in a while but it's written
right here that they're gonna be burned forever and they're always gonna be in pain and pain proves, once it gets to be really
pain, not to have any degrees. As one religious imagination has it
for hell, probably more sophisticated ones have it, it feels nice at
times and then feels ouch and so forth. "It is love. It is a hearth."
That's what I wanted to give you, how wicked a heart can be. "It
is a lantern." I'm trying to get through to myself, there are things
where you are also this but you haven't been reading them that
way. You don't yet want to know how much you're involved
with the whole thing. You don't get to love a different way when
that's going on, if you even know it's going on how your hearth
and your love can't be separated from it and aren't.

It is a lantern to read war by.
I mean it has burnd all that we value,
and we return to the burning itself,
made savage by it, warmd by it,
ears alert for the cave-lion or bear,
as a company will gather about a burning house
seeing the sparks fly up from their losses
burning,   brought together . . .
only   Love left.

So, in Hell, imagine.   All that we valued
gone up in flames.   Destroyed.
There is a great light there.

I mean the light of this war
sweeps cities, a madness, laying waste.
What remains is a hearth.
What remains is the heart. Even
out of Hell   we demand it,

Make Light. Gather about the flames
and against the night   recite
as the words dance,   dance
as the flame flickers,   burn
as the language takes for,   revive
the heat of the heart from its cold.

This fire lighting up the room
almost to a tropical heat where
the old man is dying of cancer. "You
do not know how to light a fire,"
he cries. "I will teach you
how to make a fire. So few . . nobody
today knows how to make a fire
with kerosene." This blaze
is the same kind roar of flames
that destroys in terror Korea
and we
do not know how to make a light
pouring kerosene on the already burning paper.

"What can I teach you
when there is no time for teaching?"[27]

   The fire goes all the way through. In that period, because I was
conceiving of them [poems] as part of learning the craft, and then
signal poets that really belong to my condition were the ones that
attracted and Donne's conceit I over and over again struggled,
wrestled with to get into a form. One of the things that haunts
[me] that is how fascinated I was as a child about the tempering of

---

[27] Duncan, "An Essay At War," 26-27.

metal. And we're back at fire. But you saw that the metal turns
into a light and becomes absolutely white and is plunged into water. In my curious circuits, I've almost displayed how one of
those circuits works because to me, it was incidental that I was
explaining to you about the bucket and the water in the bucket,
and then I recalled that Ian Hamilton Finlay where the vastness is
the reason there was a bucket, to catch a star. What? One thing
that's in our time, we don't think of the star. Well, it was in the
Imperium so it's always fire, those were points of fire. So it was a
realm of fire, but now we know that they're the fire we most
fear. We project with fear that a world is gonna go up. I'm not
talking about our protectiveness or anything else. We're showing
quite the contrary. Even when we think about an atomic war,
then we might mutate or anything else, then we would be radi-
ated. These are things that go on throughout the universe. That
star is a furnace, so what if I take myself in a star? I won't even
have the choice when we go into an atomic war. I mean I'll be in
a star. Where else will I have myself? You talk about strange,
who's your body or what? A furnace is almost what we described. Where else would the sun have to have the sun's self. I
always have puns. Isn't it nice to be in English where we don't
have *Soleil* and things like that. We are overly, redundantly
Christian. The son is the sun is the son is the sun and it radiates
and so forth. In this one you find your temper teaches, my temper.

    As I read last night and did my part to give voice to the poem it
becomes alarming to me how consistently being in a temper is
part of my voice in a poem. Our friendly karma things look positive. I wouldn't feel that I had a temper anger until I had only one
image on my mind, a hatchet in one hand chopping up mommy,
daddy, everybody, and all the objects around, and everything,
break everything, and I think hovering around this poetry was
always flooding it, being myself the flood that destroys Atlantis
and burning it. That comes into the voice so that it's tempered in
a temper would be the quality of what's there. With, evoked
throughout the poetry, something when you talked about water,
is, I understand from that the cult of tears. I'm very close to the

poet George Herbert.[28] As a young man and beginning to be a poet, and while I understood many of the elements in Herbert, it became clear that you weren't really there unless that area of Christianity came into a cult of tears.[29] Not a cult of tears now, of a cult of tears as I could understand it, not the mourning of the cross, but, and.I could understand part of it because I had certain occasions where I still wept. At the story of, or the ideal of those whom I found noble, I wept. It was not that they were dead or not dead and before certain works of art, visually and in music, I wept, and I have wept, when poems are being read, when the music advances. So I could be touched and I knew that, in the early world, in the physics of the early world—I'm thinking is it a Hellenic right now, but gee it's still there. And Roland when you read Roland, they weep. It's a sign of their life promise and that was why I said, when I was talking about the movie, no that's pouring forth. Pouring forth tears, now this is not sobbing, that's throwing up water, but pouring forth water and I'm talking about the weeping that comes, the streaming down here, you become a fountain. And you do potentially of blood become a fountain. I'm not talking about the whole feeling of pouring out, pouring forth; this was a sign, especially of male virility, and it's because the water was thought of—and it's before the *numen* was thought of as being the place the life was and you had an overabundance of it. You could pour it forth endlessly and remain in the power. So it was like a marvelous emotional potlatch. Since we get a reason for the weeping we don't know that we're beginning to be generous. Everybody else wanted to say I wanna hug

---

[28] Two poems, for example, from Duncan's sequence, "A Seventeenth Century Suite" derive directly from Herbert's poems. See "Jordan (I)" and "Jordan (II)," in *Ground Work: Before the War* (New York: New Directions, 1984), 76-96.

[29] Duncan wrote: "In my manly years, I weep for pain and in the pain of others, and for grief; and I weep for the power of works of art that break the reserves of my aesthetic and stand in the immediacy of first experience, and I weep for the courage of noble men. Now it comes to me that George Herbert, whose poems are addressed so directly do not have the protective remove that the poem as a work of art has or the poem as projected by the poet to his imaginary reader or hearer has, it comes to me that George Herbert wept..." ["The Truth and Life of Myth," in *Fictive Certainties* (New York: New Directions, 1985), 19-20].

you. We get to say all sorts of things which sometimes can lead to very interesting episodes, but if you can just cry. Oh, this person's being generous. Water is pouring out of them. Now we can take advantage of their generosity! Would you like to sign this check? And many other interesting things that go along on the other end of it. So I'm thinking about this water and fire. The other thing that goes on. The voice is in a temper. But grief, I'm not accounting for it, because we don't dismiss the mystery from which things are coming. On the other hand I could talk about it endlessly and it still will brood, I'm not getting rid of it by talking about it but picturing it. It's striking, too, how much I will name that grief is the primary, and yet grief, and there will be a dull figure of a stone, which weeps, or a stone which does not weep. The ultimate place—this is what Pat talked about arrest—is to be turned into a stone and that a stone weeps. The water running from the rock, the water flowing from the rock is something we see all the time. It tells us that the earth is generous, that it pours forth the thing we need not in its soil, not until it's broken down and dispersed and we can plant, but in the very place we can't plant, a rock will slip or run water and that's water, salt are the two things that are that, we gather around in order to live. I mean life forms gather around in order to live.

Because we have further business don't we? Yeah, it's stopping me as the greater thing and even me stopping me is quite—I can't have a graceful moment. Let me then read a poem in which you'll find that rock. It comes in an answer to Verlaine. I'd spoken of the blood running and Verlaine had a remarkable poem in a period when he was so excited about Christ's blood running. Now that's different from the figure of Christ on a cross in pain and the death figure. Christ's blood running is the same thing as the endless streaming of the water from the rock and, I had just written a kind of translation of Parsifal and in it was the rock. So I'm answering it when I come to this "Passages 16: The Currents":

No, Verlaine, I thirst for cool water, for the
cool of the shade tree,   I would

drink in the green of the leafy shade,

for the sweet water that wells up from under
the rock ledge, the mossy shadows

the coins of light,   shaken down
drifting dreaming in the ever-running

stream of bright water pouring over
rocks gleaming amidst the cold

current's words[30]

---

[30] Duncan refers to his poem, "Parsifal (after Wagner and Verlaine)," and then reads "Passages 16: The Currents," *Bending the Bow*, 56-57, 58.

A COLLAGE THAT SPOKE

NOR HALL

I am going to be speaking out of the pleasure of having known Robert Duncan and of having met Jess (only once, but) in their extraordinary house on the occasion of going to collect a book about the Austrian Count, Ludwig Von Zinzendorf, who shared the same border country as Dracula and Freud. Count Zinzendorf was obsessed with mystic bloodlines of human community and founded the Moravian sect in Bethlehem, Pennsylvania, where the poet H.D. grew up. Duncan in turn was obsessed with H.D. Because of her childhood, according to Robert's reading of it, I was recreating a Moravian ritual that required my having this book from his library. The ritual required that the congregation be seated in "choirs" according to their theological experience of blood—little children still bathed in the blood of birth, boys bonding by the blood of circumcision, maidens flowing from the red niche that resembled the blood flowing from Christ's side, married women, older men, etc. Everyone in a Moravian community joins the appropriate choir for each service and Robert, I am remembering—whose gender allegiance fluctu-

Nor Hall practices psychotherapy in St. Paul, Minnesota. She was a student of Robert Duncan's in the "History of Consciousness" program at the University of California, Santa Cruz, in the early 1970s. This paper was originally delivered as a slide lecture at the Walker Art Center in Minneapolis for an event called "Robert Duncan and Jess: A Grand Collaboration," on January 11, 1994.

ates according to "the lie of the words" in each sentence—sat with the Maidens.

Just as, years earlier, in the late 50's, he and Jess had been integral to a group of San Francisco poets and painters, including Helen Adam and James Broughton, that called themselves "The Maidens."

One of the advantages of knowing that you are an Orphan is that you get to chose your spiritual family. An orphan, especially in the etymological world of this poet I am remembering, is one who is deprived of parents, inheritance, and soul. Related to "robot" by the common root *orbus,* meaning "bereft," and *orbi* meaning "toil," a robot functions but is soulless, bereft, until he experiences a ritual of adoption.

In the exhibition at Wilson Library organized by Robert Bertholf, there were two astrological charts prepared by Duncan's adoptive mother and Grandmother who had been waiting for a child to appear at the right star time in history. He was adopted by earthly parents steeped in a mystic tradion that understood the claim of the ancient Orphic initiate, "I am a child of Earth and Starry Heaven, but my race is of Heaven alone."

On his last visit to Minnesota he met my daughter at a rather frantic stage of her development (age 4) when she was convinced she was an orphan. At breakfast she would suddenly look at me with suspicion and ask, "What are the names of my Dad's dogs?" or, "What is my Grandmother's first name?" Robert delighted in this attempt to trick out a true identity and did his own improvisatonal riffs on it for a week.

When Duncan was about 4 or 5, and already on to his parents' astrological predilections, he was drawing a secret picture with his crayons, just hoping that his parents would inquire about the subject matter--which they did, so that he could nonchalantly toss it off as a place he had lived once called Atlantis.
Plutarch wrote that the race of mortals, like the realm of plants, always moves in a circle. He reached out to touch his psyche's ancestors by writing letters to the ones he'd chosen.

Likewise, Duncan wrote love songs to his ancestors.

Here in this thirst that defines Beauty,
I have found kin.
Nerves tremble upon its reaches.
("The Propositions," 5)

He reached backward from fraternizing with Imagists and Tran-
scendentalists, to Cathars and Cabbalists. He was the Postman in
Finnegans Wake traveling backwards in the night through the
events he narrated.

"Door of Many Colored Glass Opend:
Imaginary Portrait #1: Robert Duncan, 1954"

With one foot pigeon-toed, "twisted," he said, "by the Daugh-
ters of Night" whose feet are turned both ways to reach into the
past and sing about the future, and with one eye crossed, he
would warn us not to guess where his gaze went, but we (as students) tried to see what he said he saw, and followed his one eye

like the Eye of Ra. In "Crosses of Harmony and Disharmony" he
describes "the double vision/ due to maladjustment of the eyes"

> the sensory line
> breaks
> so that the lines of the verse do not meet,
> imitating that void between
> two images of a single rose near at hand,
> the one
> slightly above and to the right

Jess, who worked from the same proprioceptive data, called a
collage "Dyslecstacy." Always writing out of the body, Duncan's
poetry reflects the trick of his eye, bringing doubles into focus
and the other way around, shattering focus into brilliant fragments, showing us the puzzle pieces that Jess then matches up.

"The Enamord Mage: Translation #6, 1965"

This was their magic, spellcaster to spellbinder. Duncan was the
magician of the household, bard of the books lined up to under-

score his knowledge. He adored the image of the Creator in *The Zohar* who plays creation games with the letters of the alphabet. He stands here over a bowl of cock feathers (as it says in "A Line to Jack Spicer"):

> From what we call Poetry a cock
> crows away off there at the break of something
> Always a message, always announcing

"Dazzling" was a front-runner in Duncan's stable of words. He bedazzled us. The magician in love, is love in whose presence candles burn brightly, unlike in other of Jess' paintings where burnt-out candles suggest spent energy and a dark afterlife (Auping, Catalogue essay, 51).

He is dazzled by the announcements of wonder in the room as when the hummingbird flashes through the glass of the Tiffany lamp:

> Let my awe be steady
> in the rude elements of my household
> At the window, the rose vine.
> ("Apprehensions")

The window of their domus appears as a leitmotif in Jess' work. For nearly four decades Robert and Jess were domestic partners in a joint household that treasured itself. A constant translation went on, between the library downstairs and the studio upstairs. An energetic reverence for images, visual and literary, circulated in the very air so that coming into the house as a stranger was like walking into a collage that spoke. The things of the household worked an enchantment, as any house would where the reigning deity is "a magician in Amor's likeness."

The generation and expenditure of energy in this life as it affects life to come was another of their shared concerns. Always on the look-out, the watcher (taken from *LIFE* magazine), possibly Robert, possibly Jess, in profile cuts the cards of fate and looks out over a field lit from above by a golden plutonium cloud —

Handle the cards, shuffle, the cards, cut and shuffle.
Distribute them once more upon the table.
Sometimes I am not permitted to read. . .

These are not your cards or mine.
There is an angel of the time we are reading.
To figure his likeness men have ascribed

planetary governors, angels or gods, to the hours.
There is a god of the time where the cards fall.
("Apprehensions")

—signaling the end of Jess' life as a chemist who'd once worked on the bomb, and who among us hasn't? And will the dance of childhood have a future? The pattern of their footfall echoes in Duncan's "Structure of Rime." The intended-to-be-generative ritual game like a Ring Around the Roses of moves clockwise like the sun to predict a future. Only the owl knows. Our imagination of Wisdom holds a key.

Robert and Jess pass through each others work in animal form—as the cat or the lion and eagle and owl, which Robert remarkably resembled in a dark cape and hood, with his sharp eye and feathery sideburns, and arms flapping—excited with the chance of speaking. Our set-aside hours for poetry always began with his taking a loudly ticking alarm clock out of a black briefcase. He'd set it on the table to time his own talk, and the time passed with sound so filling the room that we never heard the clock until it went off three hours later.

These classes were structured so that people could take breaks whenever necessary, but he would keep on going so inevitably that it was astonishing one day when he broke. We were meeting in the Redwood Restaurant on a rainy afternoon for which he gave us the word "mizzling," part mist, part drizzle. He was talking about the liver of Prometheus being picked by vultures. And the poem he was writing for Charles Olson who had recently died. Suddenly the words of the poem started spilling over into tears and then sobs. He burst out of the restaurant and ran into the wet forest. We sat stunned into silence until one of the women ran out after him.

Duncan found his orders in Charles Olson's announcement (from Black Mountain College in the 1950's) that a poem's structure should not be pre-determined but rather arrived at by way of one perception leading to another. Thus the focus of writing becomes what is happening in the composition. "The work of art is itself the field we would render the truth of." They called it composition by field. Robert regarded Jess' work as fieldwork, his collages as visible poems. "The poetry (the making), the science (the trained knowing), the vision (the discovery) are all one in this art: not impression, not expression, but an involvement in what is." (From an annnouncement of Jess' show at Dilexi Gallery, December, 1960.)

The opening poem in *The Opening of the Field*, "Often I am Permittted to Return to a Meadow," describes the children's circling as *poesis*:

> Lovely their feet pound the green solid meadow
> the dancers
> mimic flowers—root stem stamen and petal
> our words are,
> our articulations, our
> measures.

Off to the right of Jess' cover page collage there is a swing drawn, a forecast perhaps of a collage to come, completed in 1971. Beginning with the child in the lower left-hand corner—treating this paste-up as I would a dream, exploring the images and associations to the image—the child, overseen by observatory telescope angels, studies the text. He is nearly touched by the toe of the swinging god Eros, the boy Dionysos, Peter the Pan. (It is Pan's hour, high noon, when there are no shadows.) As in the god's mystery tradition, the teacher's foot nearly touches the seated initiate. A child reads an account of what is unfolding in the pine forest.

Jess says that using the image of the child can sometimes evoke that magical plane of childhood's imagination with its wondrous ability to infinitely connect images and stories without having to segregate everything. Imaginal space is not symbolic space. We are not talking "this equals that," but rather this leads to that—as in childhood's games, follow-the-leader, hide-and-seek which is a place where Jess and Robert found each other. As Robert Creeley said here several weeks ago, "One is let to join in the game in this art which makes it so dear."

"Midday forfit: Feignting Spell II [Spring], 1971"

While Jess was working on this piece, Robert was writing *The Truth and Life of Myth: An Essay in Essential Autobiography,* in which he strove to get at the roots of his own creative life:

> . . . its roots and depths lie in childhood or even in 'childish' things I have not put away. . . The seed of poetry springs to life in the darkness of a ground of words heard and seen that were a congregation of sounds and figures previous to dictionary meaning. The child hears the heart of speech. . . He lives in the color of things. The child (like the poet) dwells in the spirit that moves behind literal things. (13)

He then spins a paean to the bedtime story, in particular this story of Cupid and Psyche (on the swing) whose story was the first bedtime story in literature told by an old crone to a kidnapped girl stuck in a cave in Apuleius' *Golden Ass*. The story contains the stuff of soul-life. "It is important that the myth be first so familiar, so much no-more-than-an-old-story, that the poet is at home with what is most perilous" (*Truth and Life of Myth*, 27).

Cupid is the primal Eros, the First Swinger, "Major Mover/ Him I love". She is the first soul, our Psyche. Hundreds of poems and part-poems of Duncan's (do not illustrate, but) speak out of this collage. Noticing the car, for example, near the child. Duncan writes:

> You are right. What we call Poetry is the boat.
> The first boat, the body—but it was a bed.
>   The bed, but it was a car.
> And the driver or sandman, the boatman,
>   the familiar stranger, first lover,
> is not with me.
>
>   You are wrong.
> What we call Poetry is the Lake itself,
> the bewildering circling waterway—
> having our power in what we know nothing of—
>   ("Line to Spicer")

As young men, neither Duncan nor Jess thought they would live into their thirties, but when, according to Robert, "the information was in that I wouldn't kick off at age 35," he set to work. "As a youth you eat life like firewood" (class notes). At age 35, the gas jets were turned up. For Jess the bunsen burner was on, the energy of the coiled sepent admitted into the field.

"The Lord of the Heat of noon" glides across the horizon. The serpent and his fraternal allies are alert. Frogs sit erect and ready to leap. The gila monster rears like a dragon in the place of the boy-god's heart. Duncan says it's Freud's myth lying dragon-wise in our blood.

A rose blooms in her breast.

> . . . a rose that burns/the tips of their bodies, lips,/ ends of fin-
> gers, nipples. He is not wingd./ His thighs are flesh, are
> clouds/ lit by the sun . . .
>
> ("A Poem Beginning With A Line By Pindar")

Mount Rushmore ushers in the soulbride whose front is lit by
the citrus sundisk reflecting the disk that steers the motion of the
piece. Above her back a child rides across the heavens in the sun-
disc wearing the feathered falcon headdress of Horus, he-who-is-
above, kisst by a bolt, the screw from out of the blue. In Egyptian mythology he is the solar son, sometimes called by the name
of Ra whose one eye looks (Duncan-like) out of the rockwall below. Another divinity of high noon, the sun at its strongest, this
god is master of creation by masturbation—also like Pan. Siva
nearby performs the balancing act of creating and destroying,
dancing in his fire circle, marking the rhythm with a drum for
Osiris whose phallus becomes pillar holding up the sky in the
frame's left corner. God's rod rests on rowboats.

A little farther over, the hand of God holding a molecular chain
swings one side of the rope. Duncan somewhere remarks that the
Swing is the theology of Milton and Donne, sonorous, lofty, intense and sexual as is the seminal scene against the boy's thigh, the
ongoing reap and sow of love's raising grain, the radiant desire
from under ground.

The ground they've reached in their swing is the shore of
America. The Indian saw them coming. Beneath him the mushroom cloud turns black and a bubble like Bosch floats by. . . This
is the offering of the artist as alchemist trying the transmutation
of the baser elements into psychic gold. On her golden hip the
sandpainter inscribes the Pa Kua, all the tri-grams of the *I Ching*.
His instrument a loud speaker . . ."Loud hear us." (*Finnegans
Wake*)

Over the shoulder of She Soul and the Prime Mover, it is rush
hour. Everyone wants to get there. Their delight speaks in sparks
out of their highest *chakras*. Mind-blown bliss, but also a dicey
adventure going West in the covered wagon. There is no telling

what will come of it, how the fortune of Love will roll. Over-head, the entrance to Nirvana. The *boddhisattva* who sits on the rim of life will float free, tradition says, unless he/she happens to witness a copulation. That act will draw them back into life.

Eros-Amor holds the wand of life in his left hand. The rope swing becomes the flail of Osiris, the spiral thread of life carried in the sperm dance (Gk. *mitos*) or the *thyrsus* of Dionysos that suggests the saprise and seedspill of divine maleness. A tumescent tree frog announces the lightning bolt of Zeus and the molecular egg cell is struck into process. Held by Horus while overhead the directive comes from Duncan's lines, "Bells tied in the foliage/ring as the wind rises"...

Partway down the tree-trunk Chiron and Icarus show their part animal natures. One a surrogate Father, the other a winged young man who flew too high towards the sun. A minute past noon now, the phallic shadow of the plane crosses the cock perched on a puzzle. Seeing it from below, the tree watches. "Art puts eyes and ears in a place of profound worship" (Duncan quoting Burckhardt in "A Letter").

What gets forfeited, according to Duncan, is coming-to-a-conclusion. "Life is designed to prolong intensity with no teleo-logical intention. Read Schroedinger" (class notes). Turn the knob to go on through to the other side. Join the community whose reality is myth. This myth-dimension so permeated the conversa-tion and houshold habits of these two men, that, as Robert said, "You couldn't take a piss in their house without hitting a myth."

Jess wants his viewers to see what we see. Like any good dream-worker he will never tell you what a picture means. It is impossi-ble to be near their work without feeling tapped into at a level beneath your persona, drawn into the momentum of an artform that does not stop where the artist's imagination leaves off. When asked, could this be that, i.e. about the lion being the earthly par-allel of the eagle and therefore an oblique double portrait of the two of them, Jess said, "It could be, particularly if that's how you see it: Images are chosen, or more properly, they chose me be-cause of their ability to wander in meaning" (Auping, 64).

"Narkissos, 1976/1991"

One of the things I loved most about Robert was (not surprisingly) what he loved about me, and every other student he knew (including himself as student which he also always was). Mistakes! He loved and tended errors. You could not really make a mistake in his presence. Twenty-two years ago on the first day I met him I didn't know the difference between the poet H.D., Lawrence Durrell and D. H. Lawrence. He was thrilled by the mind's confabulations. There are only delightful mistakes, meaningful errors, wrong turns that lead over the border into wonder. In evolving the form of a poem, he pays insistent attention to what happens in inattentions. The process is associative. He says, "An idea is not something I have, but something that comes to me, appears to me, a thing seen" (*Truth & Life of Myth*, 29); like Jess saying that his images "find him along the way." Jess is not a scholar of the texts like Duncan, but a diver interested in following the path of a free falling image.

In the upper corner of "Narkissos," Jess's lifetime work, the diver falls through space and time scrolling through the mysteries of love and loss. This is a picture of the hermeneutics of desire told in motifs of reflection, mirroring, echoing, doubling. It is full of fortune's tellers—the sphinx, the sibyl, and fate as the cyclist bridging Pan's gap overhead. She brings up another Santa Cruz day, when we took Robert to the nude beach on the back of our motorcycles, three of us Valkyries. He rode with the woman who had run out to find him in the woods that day (whose later reflections on Jess and Robert you can read in the volume, *Tricky Cad*). His obsession at the beach was heresy and heretics, particularly the Albigensian-Manicheaen insistence on the reality of dark powers and something about the sun. Just then, heads down, plodding back to our bikes along the sandy path the setting sun intersected the horizon sending out a shaft of pink light. We looked up to see a woman walking towards us rose-cold from the frigid waters (I remember her because it was my sister) and he gasped at all the pinkness and changed the subject to Botticelli.

He used to say, "Make every event an occasion for hymns," praise or poetry. This rapture he knew often went into the dark. Narcissus, in Greek, *Narkissos*, he calls in a poem: "Nark kisses. Touched by the black stupor."

> At the bile of Narcissus you croucht to rework his mirror as if to prove a window or renew the useable surface... In the mirror next time I will wear a face that is black and trample you out. In the heart of the new poetry you are hiding. Away from me.

Eventually he arrives at his own window.

> I opend a window in the wall of the old stuff and named the bird I always hear singing a nightengale. It was the Larke, the

herald of the Mourne. No nightengale. Night's Candles are
burnt out. The Night is over
there where thou art here   the Day.

("Over There")

"Groundwork, Before the War"

Narcissus gazed where Orpheus drank. It is all covered in Jess'
cover for *Groundwork, Before the War*: the window, the candles,
the lyre, the necessary thirst of poetry's initiate who stoops to
"the well the muses command." He is given the cup "ever just
pourd"... "a memory/ kept silent come to speak." Like the god
whose instrument occupies the lower left quadrant in this paste-
up's shield, the poet thrills the inanimate world into song. Orpheus made the trees dance, he sang frozen women into fire, celebrated the mystery of the egg (aeons before James Joyce's consummate "Eggburst, Eggblend, and Eggburial"). Orpheus the
singer made the lion to lie down with the lamb, turning a wild
kingdom peaceable. The Orphic Duncan, inspired odd marriages
among us. One woman married two men who were a couple.
Women joined with women. And women and men in our group

wedded according to their feel for the same poem. This did not work in my case. In fact, there is a way in which being around Duncan spoils the idea of marriage ("Willingly I'll say it's been a sweet marriage...") because his relationship with Jess suggested an unattainable romantic fantasy of souls mated in lingual bliss, sharing an imaginally blest domicile.

Jess apparently completed "A Western Prospect of Egg and Dart" in 1988 in memory of Robert Duncan who associated his ancestors with the archetypal West. In a piece of a poem Duncan wrote for Charles Olson, "man upon whom the sun has gone down!", we find words to echo the canyon collage:

> The light that is Love
> rushes on toward passion. It verges upon dark.
> Roses and blood flood the clouds.
> Solitary first riders advance into legend.
>
> This land, where I stand, was all legend
> in my grandfathers' time: cattle raiders,
> animal tribes, priests, gold.
> It was the West. It's vistas painters saw
> in diffuse light, in melancholy,
> in abysses left by glaciers as if they had been the sun
> primordial carving empty enormities
>   out of the rock.
>
>   Snakes lurkd
> guarding secrets. Those first ones
>   survived solitude.
>   ("Poem Beginning With A Line By Pindar")

Essay quotes in the text are from the Exhibition catalogue of the Albright-Knox Art Gallery, Buffalo, New York, organized by Michael Auping, Robert Bertholf and Michael Palmer. *JESS, A Grand Collage, 1951-1993* (Buffalo Fine Arts Academy, 1993).

Robert Duncan, *The Truth & Life of Myth, An Eassay In Essential Autobiography* (Fremont, Michigan: Sumac Press, 1968).

Madeleine Burnside, *Tricky Cad*, JESS catalogue essay, Odyssia Gallery (New York) and John Berggruen Gallery (San Francisco) exhibitions, February - April, 1989.

Illustration credits:
"Door of Many Colored Glass Opend: Imaginary Portrait #1: Robert Duncan, 1954," courtesy The Literary Estate of Robert Duncan.

"The Enamord Mage: Translation #6, 1965," courtesy of the owner, Private Collection.

"Midday Forfit: Feignting Spell II [Spring], 1971," courtesy Collection of the Museum of Contemporary Art, Chicago, Gift of MCA's Collectors Group, Men's Council, and Women's Council; Kunstadter Bequest Fund In Honor of Sigmund Kunstadter and National Endowment for the Arts Purchase Grant.

"Narkissos, 1976/1991," courtesy of the Odyssia Gallery, New York.

"Groundwork, Before the War," courtesy of the artist.

WATCH YOUR STEP

CHARLES BOER

I.

The light foot hears you and the brightness begins

That is how Robert Duncan's best-known poem, "A Poem Beginning with a Line By Pindar,"[1] opens, with an elegant rendering of a line by the great Greek poet of footraces and athletic contests. But the second line is the theme not only of this but perhaps of all Duncan's poems:

god-step at the margins of thought

It is not an original theme; Ezra Pound and HD, to name but two of Duncan's supreme forebearers, wrote little that was not ever conscious of *god-step at the margins of thought*. Even when Gods are not mentioned in particular poems by these now classic poets of American literature, they are there, guiding the mind, focusing the eye, limning the voice.

---

[1]Robert Duncan, *The Opening of the Field* (New York: Grove Press, 1960), 62.

Charles Boer is the editor of this journal. He is Professor Emeritus of English and Comparative Literature at the University of Connecticut. Part II of this paper was delivered as a lecture at the Pacifica Graduate Institute in Santa Barbara, California, in November, 1995.

See, they return; ah, see the tentative
Movements, and the slow feet,
The trouble in the pace and the uncertain
Wavering!
                    (Ezra Pound, "The Return"[2])

Duncan, in turn, asks in his Pindar poem the age-old question
that visionary poets always ask, hoping Gods will answer:

Who is it that goes there?

And he clearly sees, and hears, the coming of something appari-
tional:

Where I see your quick face
notes of an old music pace the air,
torso-reverberations of a Grecian lyre.

An old music indeed. The lyre belongs to Pindar, but the theme
belongs to John Keats, who when he contemplated "a Grecian
urn" forever shaped the sentiment that the ancient world of
beauty and Gods was not only still accessible but would always
be accessible to poets and other sensitive souls.

When I first read Duncan, in the 1960s, I was not prepared for
such unremitting Romanticism. My reaction to his effulgent,
even fey verse,

crossd, athwart, fated, fey
is a man with a quick odd look,
cousin to idiocy, that strains to see
                    ["After Reading Barely and Widely"]

was that it was Romantic excess, an over-indulgence of his own
sentimentalities. He was simply over-doing it. Of the Black
Mountain poets, Charles Olson[3] was my star, and still is, but

---

[2] Ezra Pound, *Selected Poems* (Norfolk, Conn.: New Directions, 1949), 24.
[3] Charles Boer, *Charles Olson In Connecticut* (Chicago: The Swallow Press,
1975); 2nd edn., intr. by Fielding Dawson, (Rocky Mount, North Carolina:
North Carolina Wesleyan Press, 1991).

even when it came to sheer pull-out-all-the-stops sentimental pre-
ciousness I preferred the zany "I-go-here-I-go-there" poems of
Frank O'Hara, and still do.

What I find moving in Duncan's poems today, however, especially now that his work is finished, is the realization that that
almost shamelessly indulgent Romantic line of his, a line going
back at least as far as Keats, a line of strikingly eccentric men and
women who so wildly believed in the imaginal *reality* of Greek
Gods and Goddesses, has become silent. Their generation must
now begin to seem puzzling, if not altogether archaic, to younger
readers, who are, shall we say, more flattened-out? I mean, Duncan and company *really* took the Gods seriously, not just as
mythological decoration, not just as classical nostalgia, and least
of all as symbols or poetic bric-a-brac. They *believed*.

"A Poem Beginning with a Line by Pindar" is written as Duncan contemplates a painting by Goya of Cupid and Psyche. Duncan is enraptured by the beauty of the figures, especially Cupid's
as he comes to Psyche's bed:

> *The copper light*
> *falling upon the brown boy's slight body*
> *is carnal fate that sends the soul wailing*

and wail Duncan does:

> *A bronze of yearning, a rose that burns*
> *the tips of their bodies, lips,*
> *ends of fingers, nipples. He is not wingd.*
> *His thighs are flesh, are clouds*
> *lit by the sun in its going down,*
> *hot luminescence at the loins of the visible.*

The second part of the Pindar poem, for me, was always a
giveaway of the problem that "far-out" Romantics like Duncan
had with pedestrian life in America. In the second part, he reflects
dismally on the past century of American presidents since Lin-
coln. The "light foot" has become "the heavy clod," he thinks.
With a bow to Whitman's elegy, he asks:

> *What*
> *if lilacs last in this dooryard bloomd?*

The very purity of his vision—a modernist purity that has been baked spotless in the cleansing fires of Pound's furnace—cannot permit him to see anything poetic in our all too un-funky American presidents.

> *Hoover, Roosevelt, Truman, Eisenhower—*
> *where among these did the power reside*
> *that moves the heart?*

The grand Romantic tone of his own language, like a pitch in music that is just set too high for the singer to enter, could not take on America the un-beautiful, though Whitman, who had once carried it off perfectly in his own long-breathed industrial-strength tones, was one of Duncan's heroes. But Duncan's own rhapsodically-charged tongue could only ask (and of Eisenhower no less!):

> *What flower of the nation*
> *bride-sweet broke to the whole rapture?*

And when Duncan gets to

> *Hoover, Coolidge, Harding, Wilson*

his 19th century Romantic imagination can only form the lyrically exquisite but impossibly impractical question:

> *For whom are the holy matins of the heart ringing?*

And even when he lists the 19th century's own presidential characters, it is only with blanket condemnation, as if they are all one undifferentiated bearded old man:

> *McKinley, Cleveland, Harrison, Arthur,*
> *Garfield, Hayes, Grant, Johnson,*
> *dwell in the roots of the heart's rancor.*

They do? Only if you're hung up on John Keats and beauty-is-truth Romanticism, I thought, back in my youth when I was myself writing a series of poems about William Clarke Quantrill,[4] a borderlands guerilla nasty during the Civil War, and another about J. Pierpont Morgan,[5] the father of American capitalism, and even some poems about Ulysses S. Grant himself. Un-beauty is, after all, truth, too. And truth... well, you know.

It just seemed to me too grandiose, not to say pretentious even, for Duncan to declare at the end of this litany of American presidents:

> *I too*
> *that am a nation sustain the damage*
> *where smokes of continual ravage*
> *obscure the flame.*

Duncan may have thought of himself in this kind of language as keeper of the Whitmanian flame, but for me it had long gone out, replaced by a lava lamp, supplanted by the neon lights of Las Vegas (Bugsy's, not Disney's) as well as the cathode glare of television, the cinerama glow of movies, the great sweeping spotlight of the crazy American century at its midpoint. British writers, of course, hated it, French intellos pretended to hate it, American professors taught that they hated it, everybody was supposed to hate the sheer materialism of American culture. But who cared? It was *us*.

There was still, even then, *god-step at the margins of thought* but the God was Norman O. Brown's Dionysus, not his (and Duncan's and H.D.'s) Hermes; if you were still living in Europe through that period it was James Hillman's Saturn; if you were living in England it was Persephone-and-Demeter (for Sylvia Plath more Persephone than Demeter, for Elizabeth David, my own favorite post-war British writer, more Demeter than Perse-

---

[4]Charles Boer, *Varmint Q.* (Chicago: The Swallow Press, 1972).
[5]See *Tri-Quarterly 35*, ed. Michael Hamburger, Michael Anania, and Paul Auster (Evanston, Ill., 1976), 93-98.

phone). But there was, nearly everywhere, *god-step at the margins of thought* and almost *all the time*!

Decades have passed since the shifty Fifties, the sexy Sixties, the sleazy Seventies. I now see that of all the great poets that America had singing in those fabulous years, Robert Duncan's voice was closest to the Gods. That is why I had such a hard time hearing it. It was almost the kind of chant you hear in Church and pay no attention to because you know this is not real discourse or the way people speak.

You can hear it in his wonderful lecture to the Buffalo Jungians when he says of James Hillman's book, *Pan and the Nightmare*,[6] "Is Hillman also restraining himself from having rhyme, sound, and rhythm enter?"[7] What Duncan is suggesting is that Hillman's *language*, in a book on Pan that practically restores that God to a real place in the Western psyche for the first time in two thousand years, is not up to the task, is too Saturnian, too heavy. Duncan is demanding a rhythm, a flow, a swinging of the hips almost (maybe even a kicking of hooves?) that brings Pan *bodily* forth. I don't know what Hillman or others must have thought, in the audience, when Duncan made these remarks, critical of archetypal psychology's language (but of course embracing its goals). The poet was upholding a standard, *his* standard, to be sure, for invoking the Gods, and only this poet, alone of anyone alive at that time, poet or psychologist, classicist or mythologist, I see now, could get away with the claim.

That was in the early 1980s, and the high priests of imaginal reality were still, if you were in the right venue, Romantically declaiming. The 1990s, I think, which seem to be pulling in the reins all over the place, are going to miss them terribly.

---

[6]Wilhelm Heinrich Roscher and James Hillman, *Pan and the Nightmare* (Zürich: Spring Publications, 1972).
[7]See. p. 32 of this issue of *Spring*.

II.

O n a September day in the year 490 B.C., an extremely fit young man is running as fast as he can through a Greek mountain pass about 35 miles north of Sparta. He is exhausted, depressed, and frightened. Only two days before, he had crossed through this same pass on the 150 mile trip from Athens, taking the shortest possible route between the two cities. At least on the trip down from his native city he could counter the pain in his legs and his lungs with the hope that his mission would be a success. Now he is nothing but a man defeated. The Spartans had said no to his city's desperate plea for help. Sorry, they said, but they were right in the middle of the Karneia, a big festival in honor of one of their city's most important Gods, Apollo Karneios, and they could not spare anyone for at least a week.

Pheidippides, the young man, knew that would be too late. By then the Persians, thousands upon thousands of them, mindless barbarians enslaved to a stupid king, as most Greeks now thought of them, would be swarming through the Dipylon Gate at Athens, sacking the newly-formed democracy and then placing it forever under tyrannical domination. It would be only a short time after that, surely, that all of Greece would fall to their greed, becoming a mere satrap in the vast insipidity that was Persia and the past.

Pheidippides was on his way north to the plain of Marathon, where his fellow Athenians, numbering only about 9000, and a thousand other people, mostly neighbors from Platea, were encamped in the hills awaiting the Persian invasion. He knew they were expecting him to bring the news that the Spartans, the jarhead Spartans who lived for war and little else, were on the way. Now he was going to have to tell them that they were not on the way, that it would be entirely up to the Athenians to take on these hordes in hand to hand combat, each man outnumbered many times to one.

Athenians could count. They could argue all morning long about questions of justice and good, the best kind of government, the duties of a citizen, each citizen's right to a voice and a vote. Counting was essential. And now the numbers added up to a slaughter, certain defeat for their tiny democracy on the other side of Marathon's mountains. Back to tyrants, back to the petty kings who were little more than glorified killers and thieves, the power barons with pretentious families and titles, the achingly dumb past that crushed individuals who were not born to thrones or who were unwilling to cut throats to get one.

How grim the run must have been. Here was one young man on whom the future of the world was pendant, though of course he only thought of it as the future of his own city, and that was bad enough. But there was nothing in the stacked deck continually dealt by the past to think that democracies were now about to blossom no matter what. The masses of sheer dull humanity at its worst were always going to be ready to destroy a good idea. Something as delicate as the democracy that Athenians had so recently brought forth was a threat to man's most basic and brutish instinct.

Poor Pheidippides! He would have to fight at Marathon, too, when he got there. There would be no time to rest. Every single man would be needed in that insane engagement, if there would even be an engagement at all. With the message he was carrying, the Athenians might as well give up. There was no way they could win.

It was just about at this point in his desolate journey, perhaps at the point of maximum despair, perhaps at a point where he thought of not even continuing, of jumping off one of the many cliffs on Parthenion and leaving the world to its own stupefying fate, that something wonderful happened to Pheidippides, and to Athens, and to the world. All of a sudden, says Herodotus (who seems to begrudge telling the story and gives little more in his otherwise elaborately chatty and fulsome account of the Persian War), all of a sudden the God Pan "fell in with him (*peripiptei*), and addressing Pheidippides by name told him to bear this message to the Athenians: 'Why don't you pay me cult (*epimeleia*) since I am well disposed to you and have on many occasions already been useful and will be so in the future?'"[8]

---

[8]Herodotus, *The Histories*, 6. 105.

Pheidippides completed the journey and told the Athenian generals the bad news about Sparta, as well as the good news from Pan. The generals, led by Miltiades, had been debating for days whether to take on the Persians directly, hoping that the surprise alone might make some small difference in the ridiculous odds, or fight the inevitable defensive action and see how long it would take for the Persians to wipe them out in the hills. With the Spartans, of course, Miltiades' argument for a direct attack might not have seemed as suicidal as it looked. But when the first part of Pheidippides' message was spoken, and they realized they were on their own, the situation must have seemed hopeless.

Then they heard the second part of the message. Or perhaps the whole message was given in one gasping shout, but only then the second part of the message, Pan's part, got through to their ears. It must have taken a minute after all, at least, for the shock of the first part of the message to clear. And then it must have taken an even longer minute for the second part, much stranger than the first, to sink in.

"The Athenians believed Pheidippides' story," Herodotus tells us as if he did not. With the cold understatement of a scholar merely perusing his notes, a scholar who would appear smarter than his material, he adds, "And when everything was back to normal, they built a shrine to Pan under the Acropolis, and from the time his message was received they have held an annual ceremony, with a torch-race and sacrifices, to cultivate his favor." Already a new and faithless rationalism was seeping into the pens of Greek historians. The fact was, not only did the Athenians "believe" Pheidippides' *story*, they resolved *as a result of it* to fight the most famous head-on, odds-against battle in all of ancient history. And they won!

When it was over, 6400 Persians were killed, but only 192 Athenians. It would take the Persians another ten years before they would realize what had hit them. But at Marathon they had seen the future, and it was not theirs.

Perhaps we all owe Pan a little *epimeleia* to this day for his "usefulness" on that occasion, or at least those of us do who value the seeds of democracy that Athens had planted and the God had preserved. Yet many *classicists*, perhaps taking their cue from

Herodotus himself, have stopped paying it, and *mythologists*, whose misplaced sense of equality in all things mythological is now even more acute, have in recent years put all Greek myths down a notch, which is to say on a par with Bororo, Hindu, Native American, and all other manifestations of image-based thinking in the family of man. *Historians*, of course, have *never* wanted any part of the Pan story.

It matters little that this was one of the greatest moments in the history of Western civilization, this apparition of a goat-footed God on the eve of a world-transforming battle, his message of help actually making a momentous difference in the course of events that led to the saving of democracy itself. It is just that no one today—especially professional mythologists—is permitted by the increasing constraints of the subject even to take the story seriously anymore. Is the origin of democracy so small a matter, or is something wrong with mythologists?

You can take Pan's presence on the eve of Marathon "psychologically" (many ways), you can take it "symbolically," you can even take it "historically" in a twisted way (in which you account for the fact of the result but dismiss the cause as mistaken). But you cannot take it *seriously*. Something else (*if anything at all*) must have happened, the scholars say, than what Pheidippides said happened.

I hope I am not the only one who feels a certain *lese majesté* here. Somewhere in the gnarled coils and jumbled wires of mythology studies as they have spread about the classroom floor in the 1990s lies the shock of ingratitude toward this ...*symbol*(?) this ...*hallucination*(?) this ...*fiction*(?) We can barely allow ourselves anymore even to call him a God.

People on the other side of 5th century Greece were of course privileged—and privileging!—to take Pan as the splendid imaginal reality he was. Imaginal figures were "visible" to them, heard by them, touched by them. They were not, at least in their eyes, "making this up."

Seeing is believing, of course, but believing is seeing. Saying that is one way of conceding to poets and Gods without giving up your scepticism, or even your atheism. But "belief" is not what is interesting about the Pan epiphany, or even about the Gods. Seeing is. Seeing is *everything* in the bright (and dark) realms of mythology. Yet mythology today (like literary criticism), in much of its new array of theories and methods, impedes seeing. Put simply, it blocks "vision." And it does this at the same time that it pretends, with a consummate sense of distance, that this is all a problem of belief. Because belief is now out of the question for everyone, the reality of "seeing" in antiquity has now also come under attack—if you can call it an attack when scholars simply dismiss mythical visions as obvious hallucinations, and let it go at that.

So much myth discussion, even by great mythological atheists like Marx or Freud or Lèvi-Strauss, was put originally as if these were belief problems, and since that was out of the question, the discussion shifted onto the new method or strategy for reading myth where belief was not an issue.

Belief *is* not an issue. But "seeing" can be detached from belief. Seeing is a dimension just as large, just as complicated, and infinitely more important. And seeing the Gods, whatever else, has always been one of mythology's *pleasures*.

I think that Pheidippides *saw* Pan, but Miltiades and the generals, when they heard the account, saw him also. It is this second seeing that attracts me, and that I think I share as I read it. Sharing it makes me want a mythology that upholds that second kind of vision above all else, though I know that politics, then and now, is against the idea.

We are today such clever readers of political history, such masters of what universities still call political *science*, such post-Nixonian cynics extraordinaire about the least political sneeze that *everything* with a political prospect ancient or current must and will be read for who gets what, who profits from the event, who is the ultimate beneficiary of the story. *Follow the money trail*, all that Marxist-bourgeois line of reasoning. Just as we have allowed art and literature in recent years to be treated as nothing but disguised ideology, we assume that mythology must be even more so. Religion, after all, was treated this way (by Marxists) even before deconstructors got to mere poems and novels. But let us leave to others the ideology virus as it continues to ruin the pleasures of literature and art, and offer instead some obstruction to those who do the same with mythology. For mythology, ideology with its proliferating rationalisms is becoming a lethal mistake.

Miltiades and his generals, for example, are now forever subject to the political reading (rather than the mythological one). They are portrayed as accepting Pheidippides' story because it can be used for political gain. The contemporary classicist thinks he sees the plot, and Herodotus has already laid a suitably sceptical groundwork for this kind of approach. Thucydides, furthermore, only a generation later, hammered that nail even deeper in the coffin of myth for all historians to come. Perhaps that is what "history" is, or was intended to be by the Greeks who invented it as a genre of narration: a mere deconstruction of myth, with an eye as well to privileging the politics of advantage. (Power-greed as the ultimate motive of human life; the scarlet letter of "naive" on anyone who refuses to accept this viewpoint.)

Certainly with the coming of history, the decline of "seeing" mythical events set in. The Ionian philosophers[9] who started the revolution were all *atopos* (either exiles or wanderers) and their placelessness was a factor in their own decline of "seeing" (once you leave the sites, the "sights" leave you). Alienation was the source of philosophy as the deracinated questioned their native myths. In the two hundred years from Pythagoras to Epicurus (both exiles from Samos) imaginal reality was the target of targets.

Yet reality for the Greeks had an imaginal base from the beginning, and *it never lost this base* even after the Ionian revolution in thought and the arrival of philosophy in the 5th century. The images changed, and the imaginal certainly moved much further back in the philosophical head. But it did not go away, even for most intellectuals.

Imaginal reality is a world where the figures of story, including divinities, are treated as having the same visibility as anything else you consider to exist. Tradition is a better word for it, but a word so totally exhausted today that it only serves to turn people off from the very idea of what it represents. Imaginal reality was

---

[9]For a summary, see especially Bernard Frischer, *The Sculpted Word* (Univ. of California Press, Berkeley, 1982), 53-54.

once part of the very training of the Greek heroic class, the aristocratic tradition which we see in the *Iliad* when Peleus, the father of Achilles, turns his son over to Phoenix for education. In addition to learning how to perform heroic deeds, Peleus told the teacher to make his son a good "orator of myths" (it is often badly translated as "giver of advice," *muthon rheter, (Iliad 9.443)*. This was education for the real world of images, an education in myth so that you would speak and act well (including thinking) in accord with a reality where Gods interacted with people.[10] You learned myth as a basis for envisioning action, as a way of explaining your world and its values. If something extraordinary happened to you—and it was bound to, so richly imaginal was the world—you would know how to account for it, in what terms to put it. You would know where to place your experience in the vast panorama of Gods and Goddesses, heroes and nymphs, satyrs and goat-footed figures that was the agreed-upon imaginal reality of your world. You were not forced to an abstract question of ethics or non-visible values.[11] And best of all, everyone knew what you were talking about.

We do not know anything whatsoever about Pheidippides besides what Herodotus says about him. Was he an aristocrat? Was he a slave (improbable)? Was he just the fastest guy they could find? Probably the latter, for Herodotus describes him as "a professional runner still in the practice of his profession," yet the chances of his being part of an imaginal reality system of the kind Achilles was himself introduced to by Phoenix are better than average, especially if he was an ordinary citizen with no intellectual credentials. In Pheidippides' day, only intellectuals were beginning to break with the system, and only a few of those.

---

[10]As Marcel Detienne observes of this kind of orator, he was "neither the professional orator of the fourth century nor the mature citizen when he takes the floor and discusses projects in the Prytaneum but a man who knows how to express his opinion and to speak appropriately and when necessary. In this category as well as in many others *muthos* is a synonymn for *logos,* throughout the sixth century and even in the first half of the fifth." Marcel Detienne, *The Creation of Mythology* (Chicago: Univ. of Chicago Press, 1986), 45.

[11]The reader who has never read of these distinctions in Greek heroic behavior could find no better place to start than with Eric Havelock's *Preface to Plato* (Cambridge: Harvard UP, 1963).

At any rate, Herodotus was himself already undercutting what Pheidippides *saw*. He is the first to dismiss myths and stories—the fictional—from history even as he invents this new prose way of narrating events. Herodotus is still very much a tale-teller, but he makes it clear that he only wants "to put on record" such stories. "My business," he says at one point, "is to record what people say, but I am by no means bound to believe it—and that goes for this book as a whole."[12] The fact that he puts a lot of such stories on record led some readers (and especially his most important reader, Thucydides) to underrate his intelligence. Thucydides himself, with the first and most ruthless of historical pens, goes all the way toward eradicating "myth" from his account of the Pelopponesian War. He is not going to be anybody's fool.

He says of his views:

> Assuredly they will not be disturbed either by the lays of a poet displaying the exaggeration of his craft, or by the compositions of the chroniclers that are attractive at truth's expense; the subjects they treat of being out of the reach of evidence, and time having robbed most of them of historical value by enthroning them in the region of legend...The absence of romance in my history will, I fear, detract somewhat from its interest...[13]

There are no recorded Pan appearances in the Pelopponnesian War, although whether this is because they did not happen to people, and people did not see the God offering help to Athens again as he did at Marathon, or because they simply were not recorded, cannot be said. We can be sure, though, that if there were such epiphanies from the Gods, our source, Thucydides, has already screened them out for the "history" we have to accept from his hands. He has of course screened a lot of other things for us, inevitably, in his pursuit of delivering "the truth."

In the first century, B.C.E., a Greek historian named Dionysus of Halicarnassus wrote an essay on Thucydides in which he said that there were many historians in antiquity at the time of the

---

[12]Herodotus, 7. 152.
[13]Thucydides, *The Peloponnesian War*, trans. John H. Finley, Jr. (New York: Random House, 1951), 14.

Pelopponnesian War. He gives over a dozen long-forgotten names, from Eugammon of Samos to Xanthus the Lydian. Then he says:

> Those historians adopted the same principles in the choice of arguments and had more or less the same talent, some presenting the history of the Greeks, others those of the Barbarians without connecting them but separating them into peoples and cities and publishing them independently of each other thus pursuing the same single goal: to bring to the knowledge of everyone the memorial traditions (*mnemai*) which were preserved by the natives, by peoples and by cities, whether they be written (*graphai*) traditions deposited in sacred or profane places. Those written traditions-memoirs they brought to everyone's attention, just as they received them and without striking anything out. And among those traditions were certain fictitious accounts (*muthoi*), subjects of very ancient belief, and certain unexpected events such as are represented in the theater and which seem very senseless to our contemporaries.[14]

So there was a world of *mythoi* that the more progressive "historians" of the 5th century, and Thucydides most of all, protected us from and are now forever lost. The Pan epiphany in Herodotus would have been one of them had not Herodotus recognized that it was important for us to know that this epiphany influenced the generals in *his* war. Thus it was a *mythos* he would report even though he, too, was among the newly sophisticated out to screen "history" from such events. Herodotus in this case was more intelligent than Thucydides (who was contemptuous of his predecessor), or at least more pragmatist, in that he recognized that the consequences mattered even if their origin was "false."

It is usually said that Thucydides was writing to analyze political action. John Finley, one of his most distinguished modern critics, says, "His first purpose is to elucidate the motives, policies, decisions and acts of leadership which dictated the course of the war..."[15] But if this meant ruling out epiphanies of the di-

---

[14]See W. Kendrick Pritchett, *Dionysius of Halicarnassus. On Thucydides.* (San Francisco: Berkeley UP, 1975), 50-55.
[15]Finley, x.

vine—like Pan—to runners carrying important messages to generals—then Thucydides was not only leaving mythology out of his
analysis—a failing that we could never accuse Herodotus of—but
psychology as well. If Herodotus had not told us of Pan's apparition, we would have concluded the generals made their momentous decision in a far darker light than they did (the kind of light
we have to believe Thucydides' generals are always behaving in, a
mythless light, a *Godless* light). In this sense the "manual for future statesmen" that Thucydides was writing—if its unspoken
agreement was that they should discount on the face of it all messages from Gods—was giving them bad advice indeed.[16]

Thucydides was himself a general, though a losing one in his
war, unlike the Greek generals at Marathon. (He let the Spartan
general Brasidas take Amphipolis.) He spent 20 years in exile as a
result. Finley compares him to Dante as an exile obsessed with
politics, but they could not be more antithetical, the poet grasp-
ing every myth, every tale for a fantastic image to pound his case
against the Catholic Church, the general trying ever so hard to do
his part for the new aura of science sweeping over Greece: pains-
takingly documenting, for example, the plague in Athens, for
"future usefulness" to any budding Hippocrates out there, and
with meticulous concern for calendar chronologies (the Greek
states all kept different calendars) as linear time now pretty much
demolishes "once upon a time" tales. Myths are what Thucydides
was most writing *against*, their aura of popular gullible-
mindedness now being utterly offensive to him.

The imaginal base of Greek reality significantly extended into
what they called, for the first time, *psyche* or soul. By the time

---

[16]It may not be too irrelevant to report here an incident that occurred in one of
the late Professor Finley's own classes, at Harvard University in the Fall of 1962,
during the Cuban Missile Crisis. Finley was in the middle of one of his grand
lectures (on Sophocles, as I recall) when the Classics Department secretary suddenly appeared at the door and delivered a message. The professor excused himself and said he would return immediately. About fifteen minutes later, he returned, resumed the lecture almost in mid-sentence, but then looked up over his
glasses with a twinkle at the class to explain, as if in an aside, that the President
of the United States, on the telephone, had wanted a quotation from Thucydides
on the great Athenian statesman, Pericles. (John Finley, 1904-1995)

Heraclitus used the word, *psyche* was on its way out as something as universal as breath and breathing, and on its way in as the new special home for the inward imagination, with all its subjectivities and inexact emotional portrayals of ideas as images. By the time "psychology" came along in the 19th century to contain the imaginal in an even larger (and much more mechanical) framework, seeing the Gods on the *real* plane of human life was but a nostalgic (fictional) experience conceded only to people like John Keats, that is, to poets; or, worse, to crazies; or, best, to children. The big boys, then, as with Thucydides before, discounted the imaginal. Psychology, because it was now in an antiseptic environment, became as a result a successful container for what *psyche* had proposed originally to contain but messily. Thucydides, had he lived in the 19th or 20th centuries, would gladly have accomodated his studies to psychology's requirements. But in the 5th, with its *images* running amok all over the new "historic" place, it was a subject for suckers. It was *myth*!

Without giving the Gods any further thought—certainly without paying them any *epimeleia*—some classicists today proceed in discussing the subject as if a naive rationalism were once again not only their prerogative but simply to be taken for granted as the only sensible way to deal with the subject. Robert Garland, for example, comments on the Pan epiphany to Pheidippides almost apologetically, in a book that studies how new Gods made inroads into cities where they had no previous cult:

> From a rationalist viewpoint, it would hardly have been surprising if, exhausted, deoxygenated, isolated and utterly despondent due to the failure of a mission upon which Athens' whole survival was believed so heavily to depend and into which he had injected all his physical, emotional and spiritual energies, he thought he saw a divine being, half-god and half-man, whose natural habitat was precisely the kind of bleak and deserted landscape which he was currently traversing.[17]

This sounds like the preliminary paragraph to a chapter that will then show the opposite. We wait for the word "But..." to tell us

---

[17]Robert Garland, *Introducing New Gods* (Ithaca, N.Y.: Cornell UP, 1992), 50.

then how truly surprising the event was. But no such chapter comes. The author's rationalism has settled on the physiological and "psychological" condition of the runner as a sufficient explanation of the phenomena, and proceeds to discuss the politics of the Athenian priests in terms of the possible extent of their greed to get the Pan cult set up in Athens.

It is a rationalism that does not even question the details of the epiphany. Pheidippides had said that Pan "fell in with him (*peripiptei*)." The rightness of that word is the kind of thing that makes even a prosecutor suspect the witness is telling the truth. It is the sort of word that seems to have come from Pheidippides rather than Herodotus. Or it is Herodotus knowing that Athena, Zeus, or Apollo are not the kind of deities that "fall in with" people. They sneak up on them (Athena), they deceive them in disguise (Zeus), and they chase them or shoot at them "from afar" (Apollo), but only Pan—who seems always available, whether to forlorn nymphs like Echo or even to Psyche herself at the moment she was about to jump to her death—only Pan can *peripiptei*, right in step.

It is a rationalism that does not ask, why Pan and not some other God? Mountains were as much Zeus' territory as Pan's (though more in the sense of their Olympian majesty than their goatish roughness), and Artemis in particular ranged these wilds (though more pristinely, and usually at a good distance from sweaty runners), and Athena herself might even have made the trip from Athens (by air of course) since it was her city that needed protection. If this is all just a matter of 20th century oxygen deprivation, would not any God do?

If determinism is the outlook, why not say that the landscape itself determined the God? There are goats all over Greek mountains, and their suggestiveness of a goat-footed God is easy. Environment is certainly a part of everyone's imaginal reality, no matter where they're from. But that is a rationalism, too, letting the fantastic go as merely a matter of the animal *suggesting* the image of the God.

Environment determines much of imaginal reality, but imaginal reality—a very *loaded* and (as they used to say of a certain kind of logic) *dirty* process—determines environment. This "bleak and deserted landscape" (to Garland) may not look that way to me if I am a Greek goatherd (or an Athenian runner) anymore than Las Vegas looks sleazy to me if I am a devoted gambler. (Or conversely, the Greek landscape—*because of* Greek imaginal reality—was once magnificent. It is significant, now that its imaginal reality has changed, that Athens has become one of the worst polluted automobile exhaust wastes in all of Europe, its precious statues and architecture deteriorating at the same shameless rate as its civic imagination.)

The landscape may have suggested Pan to Pheidippides, but Pan was *there*, too. *How* he was there is of course where all the trouble lies, especially if one wants to go beyond merely saying that it was through hallucination, or beyond saying that a belief system (Greek religion) sponsored his being there, and even beyond saying (with Hillman's archetypal psychology) that if we *deliteralize* Pan we can best understand his being there. *Being there*: there's nothing like it.

Imaginal reality is more than merely seeing Gods and Goddesses and personified figures of the imagination (or unconscious), grand though that is. Imaginal reality sees *everything* in images, the landscape as well as the strange figures in the landscape. It is larger than what the archetypal psychologists usually mean by *soulscape* or similar Romantic words. It is encompassed only by that much less saleable word, *reality*. It was life itself.

But back to Garland, who writes from the new academic perspective of a *de-imaginalized* realism and thinks he is supported by something called "psychology:"

One way of interpreting Pheidippides' encounter with Pan, therefore, is to see it as a way of coming to terms with the otherwise insurmountable gap between superhuman effort and negligible result. To put it in the language of modern psychology, the god of Pheidippides' imagining compensates the runner for his wasted effort by supplying him with a positive message to offset the negative one received from the Spartans. Pan's message is thus an expression of the keenfelt desire of the runner's own ego—his desire, that is, to be the vessel of Athens' salvation. Or as Borgeaud expresses it: "The herald exteriorises as an objective fact a voice that is actually only a projection of his wish."[18]

By "modern psychology" then, we have to conclude that all Garland means is Freudian ego compensation and all Borgeaud means is Freudian wish-fulfillment dreaming. (Gibsonian[19] psychology, for example, a dominant approach to perception theory for the past twenty years, would scoff at such "in the head" explanations altogether and would show how Pheidippides was merely (or not *merely* in the least!) "picking up" images from the landscape; Jungian psychology would begin "in the head" too, but instead of reducing Pheidippides' imagination to a mechanical "ego compensation" scheme, would frame his experience in the context of existing archetypes. Here I wish only to remind the reader that there are many other "modern" psychologies than the "house psychology" still used by some humanist academics when they feel a need to give a psychological credential to their work.)

To try to explain away a great mythological event of the past by adopting the myth-system of the father of psychoanalysis (Freud), committed as it is to a reductionism of all myth, is an unsatisfactory bargain. Paul Veyne, in his book, *Did The Greeks Believe In Their Myths?*, has already made this point about Freudian mythology interpreting Greek mythology:

> It is amazing that the strangeness of his work startles us so little: these tracts, unfurling the map of the depths of the psyche, without a shred of proof or argument; without examples, even for purposes of clarification; without the slightest clinical illustration; without any means of seeing where Freud found all that or how he knows it. From observing his patients? Or, more likely, from observing himself?[20]

---

[18]Garland, 63.

[19]For Gibsonian psychology, see especially Peter N. Kugler and Michael T. Turvey, *Information, Natural Law, and the Self-Assembly of Rhythmic Movement* (Hillsdale, N.J.: Erlbaum Associates, 1987). See also, Peter Kugler and Charles Boer, "Archetypal Psychology Is Mythical Realism," *Spring 1977*, 131-152.

[20]Paul Veyne, *Did The Greeks Believe In Their Myths?* (Chicago: Univ. of Chicago Press, 1988), 30.

There would be nothing wrong with the Freudian explanation of Pan's apparition if it left us, after all the mechanical gears of his compensation theory have ground, *something* of the God Pan, some hairy shred of this fabulous goat-headed divinity who can persuade Greek generals to take tremendous odds and win. But the sad fact is that once the Freudian formula has been allowed to chew up the myth, classicists like Garland are left with nothing. Pan is banished from the discussion. The Athenians won the battle all by themselves. The mythic perspective—which is what literally deterred the argument for flight and won the battle!—is not even to be taken seriously:

> The intervention attributed to the gods at Marathon offers perhaps the most complete explanation in Greek history of a military victory won against all odds. As such it serves as a valuable object lesson for the variety of ways in which human life is subject to divine influence at moments of crisis. In the language of religion the victory at Marathon was accomplished by the uncommon valor of the Marathonomachoi, by Persian hubris, and by the interventions of gods and heroes. All of this is merely another way of saying that it was due to the extremely high morale and discipline of the Athenians, the over-assurance of the Persians, the peculiarly advantageous seasonal and climatic conditions, and the fact that the Athenians were fighting on home ground for everything which they owned. Who won the battle of Marathon? The gods and heroes of Athens. Or, if you prefer, an extraordinary concatenation of circumstances favorable to the Athenian side. It is ultimately a matter of perspective.[21]

Some perspective! Psychology, and a poor one at that, has absorbed religion and myth, and presto, we have the great battle of Marathon reduced to "morale." What, after all, is this "morale" (a word one would have thought was abandoned forever on the unholy battlefields of Vietnam in the 1960s, where generals like Westmoreland kept inflating it for public consumption and grunts kept swearing it was all a myth)? The Athenians were surely scared to death! By "morale" Garland can only mean Pan's

---

[21]Garland, 63.

inspiration for the Athenians—there was simply *nothing else* going for them. But then why not call it that? The reason he does not, as Garland explains at the end of his book, tells all too much about the *faithless* state of classical studies at the present time:

> Our inability to take the Olympian gods seriously [!] puts us at a comparable disadvantage [to people who can't understand why the followers of the Ayatollah Khomeini were so moved at his funeral] in undertaking a study of Greek religion, since we tend to assume a *priori* that the Olympians are and never were "real" gods. What I have tried to do in this book, therefore, is to accord Athenian religion as much respect (reverence would be too strong a word) as I am capable of demonstrating to any system of belief which does not number me among its adherents. It may in conclusion be salutary to bear in mind that gravitation does not exist either, even if we seem to feel its effects, for Einstein's theory of General Relativity now postulates that what Newton described as gravitation is actually the consequence of a geometrical configuration which directs lesser bodies towards larger ones. Yet belief in the Olympian gods and the theory of gravitation have in their different ways assisted the human mind in accounting for its experience of the world, and the fact that they have only proved provisional in no way diminishes their usefulness. When the Greeks attributed their salvation to a new and previously unacknowledged deity, as they did constantly throughout their history, what they were doing, I submit, was not unlike discovering a new scientific formula. The goal of Greek religion, like that of post-classical physics, was at bottom relatively modest: it signified an attempt to achieve a limited understanding of the constrained randomness of Chaos.[22]

As for gravitation, Einstein did not claim that it did not exist, rather that Newton's understanding of the effect was too small for the purposes of Einstein's own physics. And if that is to be the analogy for Garland's "inability to take the Olympian Gods seriously," it would be interesting to observe him walking, falling, or otherwise dealing with "gravity" on a post-classical level.

---

[22]Garland, 173.

I am picking on Garland here and throughout because he is a case of something that is becoming increasingly apparent in classical studies: the classicist who can no longer find any *use* for the Gods, but who wants you to know that he knows fully that the Greeks did. *Epimeleia* is no longer being paid, and by the people who owe it the most!

Garland is convinced, like many mythologists today, that Greek myth is beyond our experience, that our own understanding of the world is different from the Greek (and more cynical), and that we must factor in our cynicism (to offset their religion) if we are to understand them:

> Yet to treat Athenian religion *merely* as an extension of her political and social aspirations, and to extrapolate from it *merely* a coded commentary on Athens's relationship with herself and the outside world, is to miss half the point, because religion was not an epiphenomenon of a state's temporal aspirations. Any investigation of Athenian religion, if it is not to founder upon our own rationalising presuppositions, must give appropriate weight to the identity of Athenian religious sensibilities. From a Christian or merely modern perspective Athenian religion appears patently fraudulent since self-interest formed an essential and indissoluble part of its *raison d'etre* and *modus operandi*. It is tempting to regard it as little more than a rich hunting ground for cynical, manipulative and ambitious politicians whose sole objective was to exploit a credulous and ignorant populace. Exploitation, cynicisim, and manipulation were indeed prominent features of Greek religion, as they have been of religious systems throughout history. What marks out this system from others, however, is that it treated worldly success as wholly commensurate with divine favour and patronage. We therefore need to acknowledge that we are dealing with a conception of the world which is entirely different from our own experience and understanding of it. It is precisely because human life was so inextricably bound up with the divine that it is so difficult to discover the underlying motives behind the introduction of a new god.[23]

---

[23]Garland, 172-173.

The Calvinist Protestant reader, and the ancient Hebrew or modern Jewish reader, may well wonder how "self-interest" distinguishes ancient Greek religion from their own. If "worldly success as wholly commensurate with divine favour and patronage" is what marks the Greeks' as opposed to other religions, it would have come as news to John D. Rockefeller, Sr., J. Pierpont Morgan, and even that consummate robber baron Jay Gould, to name but a few American beneficiaries of the Calvinist faith who often reflected on how God favored them.

The trouble with this scholar's approach is clear in his last sentence, where "the underlying motives of the introduction of a new god" cannot fathom the God's own introduction of himself. In this view, Pan simply did not appear to Pheidippides. Gods do not exist, except in the (deoxygenated) imagination of the "ignorant populace" or in that of (mostly cynical) political operators. The great God Pan is, indeed, dead. Again!

This new breed of classicist, in routinely dismissing the reality of Gods for his own world, no longer even grants the imaginal *existence* of the Gods *in the past*. Up until now it has always been taken for granted that it was as easy for Pheidippides, in 490, to have seen Pan, as it would have been for Achilles to have seen Athena at the Trojan War (he was under great pressure, too!). Seeing the Gods was what people who believed in Gods did. But today all this seeing and imaginal activity is itself being categorically and *subtly* dismissed. A real level of religious life—one that even the atheist used to allow as "real" because the system created it—is being denied. This is a new and far deadlier rationalism than the kind so often pinned on the likes of another British classicist, H. J. Rose, who once argued that Homer's Trojan horse was "quite conceivably a confused reminiscence of some Oriental siege-engine."[24] The new rationalism is suggesting that Greeks even in *their own religious period* did not *see* the Gods.

---

[24]Rose is the author of the following notorious passage in a still widely disseminated *Handbook of Greek Mythology* (New York: Dutton, 1960, first published in 1928). "The Greeks at their best were sane, high-spirited, clear-headed, beauty-loving optimists, and not in the least other-worldly. Hence their legends are almost without exceptions free from the cloudiness, the wild grotesques, and the horrible features which beset the popular traditions of less gifted and happy

The imaginal reality of Greek myth is slowly being dismissed because there is no imaginal reality *acceptable* in academic thought today. It is not a deliberate move—I doubt that it is even a conscious one—but rather a sliding, a slipping, the logical residuum of so much anti-image and anti-myth thought in the past twenty years.

It nonetheless amounts to a major change in thinking about Greek myth, different from any in even the first half of the 20th century, when Freudians and Marxists were more influential than they are in the second half, but when the *images* of Greek myth were even for these critics never questioned *in themselves*. Pheidippides was granted his vision of Pan because Pheidippides was living inside a religious system which (naively) imaged such Gods. Now, it is pretended, not only do we know better (we *always* knew better), now the Gods themselves are dismissed not just on the level of naiveté—that was always understood— but as delusions, as mere oxygen deprivation, when it is not a case of outright political conning. Neither Garland, nor any other classicist to my knowledge, has actually argued a case for discounting the Greek imagination itself. It is only that they give Greek myth—and the Gods—such shorter and shorter shrift (because their own admitted use for myth is so low or non-existent) that things have now descended to this imageless level. And it is a descent—we are far from Martin Nilson's rationalist but nonetheless comprehensibly respectful treatment of Greek religion here, as we are far from Karl Kerenyi's much deeper psychological appreciation. And we are, needless to say, eons below the giants of Greek mythical thought after Nietzsche, scholars like Farnell, Rohde, Jane Harrison or A. B. Cook, whose monumental works

---

peoples. Even their monsters are not very ugly or uncouth, nor their ghosts and demons paralyzingly dreadful. Their heroes, as a rule, may sorrow, but are not broken-hearted; on occasion they are struck down by adverse fate, but not weakly overwhelmed; they meet with extraordinary adventures, but there is a certain tone of reasonableness running through their most improbable exploits. As for the gods and other supernatural characters, they are glorified men and women, who remain extremely human, and on the whole neither irrational nor grossly unfair in their dealings." Rose, 14.

now seem quaint or even passé precisely because of their own deep sense of the Greek imaginal experience.

But the new rationalism is not even on the level of an atheist like Marx, who, in his own doctoral dissertation on Epicurus actually argued for the *reality* of the Gods as images![25]

---

[25]Karl Marx's dissertation at the Royal Frederick William University in Berlin in 1841, when he was 23 years old, was entitled "The Difference Between the Democritean and the Epicurean Philosophy of Nature." Hegel had treated the materialist philosophers of antiquity with considerable scorn, so Marx, already an atheist at 23, was making a bold move against what he saw as the superstitious sources of religion, especially Hegel's sophisticated presentation of an intellectual (humanist) religion. Since much of the attitude of the new rationalism that I am criticizing is a kind of late (1970s and 80s) residue of second-hand Marxism (as well as a residue of second-hand Freudism), the record should state Marx's own position on imaginal reality. Claiming that Hegel has turned all the proofs for the existence of God upside down, rejecting them in order to justify them, Marx, in his dissertation, asks, "What kind of clients are those whom the defending lawyer can only save from conviction by killing them himself?" (Hegel had said, "Since the accidental does *not* exist, God or Absolute exists.") But then Marx takes on the question of the imaginal: "The proofs for the existence of God are either mere hollow tautologies. Take for instance the ontological proof. This only means: 'that which I conceive for myself in a real way (*realiter*) is a real concept for me, something that works on me.' In this sense *all gods,* [emphasis Marx], the pagan as well as the Christian ones, have possessed a real existence. Did not the ancient Moloch reign? Was not the Delphic Apollo a real power in the life of the Greeks? Kant's critique means nothing in this respect. If somebody imagines that he has a hundred talers, if this concept is not for him an arbitrary, subjective one, if he believes in it, then these hundred imagined talers have for him the same value as a hundred real ones. For instance, he will incur debts on the strength of his imagination, his imagination will *work, in the same way as all humanity has incurred debts on its gods.* [emphasis Marx]. The contrary is true. Kant's example might have enforced the ontological proof. Real talers have the same existence that the imagined gods have. Has a real taler any existence except in the imagination, if only in the general or rather common imagination of man? Bring paper money into a country where this use of paper is unknown, and everyone will laugh at your subjective imagination. Come with your gods into a country where other gods are worshipped, and you will be shown to suffer from fantasies and abstractions. And justly so. ...*That which a particular country is for particular alien gods, the country of reason is for God in general, a region in which he ceases to exist.* [emphasis Marx]." Karl Marx and Friedrich Engels, *Collected Works*, Vol. 1, (New York: International Publishers, 1975), 103.

How did classical studies, and classical mythology in particular, get to such a sterile and glum state of affairs? Surely Freud cannot be *entirely* blamed, because few classicists seem to have actually read him beyond—if even that—*The Interpretation of Dreams*.[26] Is it the influence of Claude Lèvi-Strauss, whose scorn for *Greek* myths is so notorious? And yet a reading of anything from *Tristes Tropiques* to *Mythologiques* suggests a man at least moved by the mythical imagination of *sociological* mankind. These figures would never dismiss the mythic experience they devoted so much analysis to as anything so demeaning as oxygen deprivation or hallucination.

Is it just the debunking, rationalist, progressive-materialist, atheist-relativist base of late 20th century scholarship, like a kind of rolling blob of "sophistication," finally wearing down even classicists? What has the revolution in mythology studies done to them? For while the "progressive" part of this revolution is out to put these Gods in their place because they are Greek (and the missionary part because they are not Christian, or Hindu or African or Native American), the classicists seem to be coming to the table with the weakest hand of all, that such figures are Gods in the first place.

III

The light foot hears you and the brightness begins

god-step at the margins of thought

In the third and fourth parts of his Pindar poem, Robert Duncan turns to his two living heroes, the poets Ezra Pound and Charles Olson. Pound is:

father of many notions,
                Who?

---

[26]I have certainly taken all the potshots at Freud and Freudians that anyone could possibly be entitled to in a lifetime, and will forfend here. See James Hillman and Charles Boer, *Freud's Own Cookbook* (Harper and Row, New York, 1985).

let the light into the dark? began
the many movements of the passion?

Olson is the poet of "West" (the title of one of his works) whose
Maximus Poems map the city of Gloucester, Massachusetts' history as a projection of events that started in the mythlands of the
2nd millenium B.C.E. Duncan calls upon him, as I read the
poem, as "the hero who struggles east..." Duncan is himself far
west of Olson's Gloucester, in San Francisco, California:

West
from east men push.

He remembers the California west of his own ancestors, America
in its primordial state:

This land, where I stand, was all legend
in my grandfathers' time: cattle raiders,
animal tribes, priests, gold.
It was the West. Its vistas painters saw
in diffuse light, in melancholy,
in abysses left by glaciers as if they had been the sun
primordial carving empty enormities
out of the rock.

Duncan is thinking about how far he has himself come on the
earth from Greek images and stories like the Cupid and Psyche
myth that haunts him. He has come to America! But the poem
itself keeps returning to Psyche, the woman of myth who is also
the soul of Duncan himself:

Psyche travels
life after life, my life, station
after station,
to be tried

The footfall that began the poem, the light foot that is from Pindar but is as well the very unPindaric light foot of Duncan's own

new verse line, is also the step of the God who is ever at the margins of thought. How deeply this poet cherishes the image!

> *that foot informd*
> *by the weight of all things*
> *that can be elusive*
> *no more than a nearness to the mind*
> *of a single image.*

Duncan, melancholy in America, and Psyche at the edge of the cliff ready to jump were it not for the grace of Pan: in this marvelous rhapsody of his own despairing psyche, the poet takes us from Greek runners to Goya's images, from American presidents to "the mystery of Love." He has gone so far out, away, off, it has brought him that priceless, ineffable and, yes, beautiful thing, "god-step at the margins of thought."

> *And the lonely psyche goes up thru the boy to the king*
> *that in the caves of history dreams.*
> *Round and round the children turn.*
> *London Bridge that is a kingdom falls.*
> *We have come so far that all the old stories*
> *whisper once more.*

Oh, Robert, ask not for whom the holy matins of the heart are ringing. They ring for thee.

HORSES AND HEROES

JAMES HILLMAN

T he delicacy, the gentility—that's what we often miss, seized as we are with the thundering hooves, the muscled flanks, the headstrong force of a galloping Arab, ears laid back, neck stretched into the wind. But the delicacy of a horse's lips, its lashes, its throat and leg bones, the sweetness of its stable smell, the nuzzling. "...her long ear/That is delicate as the skin over a girl's wrist," as James Wright writes about horses in his poem, "The Blessing." And, impressed as we are with the plow-horse, the dray-horse, the pack-horse, we forget how much they belong to the airy element as if all horses had wings, flying through the wind, tail streaming, nostrils flared wide, the air rushing through their innards—wheezing, whinnying, panting, rumbling, snorting, farting.

The young heroes of Greek myths rode their horses into the air: Bellerophon on Pegasus, Phaethon driving his father's chariot of the sun, Hippolytos racing off the roadside to his death. They couldn't hold their horses, and crashed.

Usual symbolism attaches the horse to the earth and the sea, to Poseidon, the sea-god: the waves, the horse's mane; its stallion thrust, the God's unstoppable power; its hoof, the magic of fertility. When this ferocious strength is perceived in a woman, the

James Hillman is the Senior Editor of this journal. This paper is an excerpt from a forthcoming book, *Now You See Them — Now You Don't: Animal Images and Dreams*, Text by James Hillman, Images by Margot McLean (Chronicle Books, San Francisco, 1997).

horse is demonized into the witch's steed, the nightmare, the pan-icky madness of a runaway.

Although horses may be work-horses and farm-horses pulling their loads of civilization, dream horses still carry heroes on their backs, both in the images of dreams and in the invisible myths that accompany these images.

Crusaders and Conquistadores; Mongols and Huns; Moham-med's faithful, riding to convert the vast expanses of the Arabian world; Apaches in Arizona, Gauchos in Patagonia; the cavalry advancing into native lands, followed by the Iron Horse on rail-road tracks. All the extraverted push into distance accomplished on horseback. Heroes and Saviors: Paul Revere, the Pony Ex-press, Teddy Roosevelt's Rough Riders, the dashing escapes of Kings and Queens. Washington, Lee, Sheridan—statues in the parks of bronze men sitting bronze horses. Napoleon's horses dragging an army's materiel across Poland to Moscow, their car-casses stiff in the snow; and Hitler's horses, tens of thousands, bearing the Wehrmacht on their backs. Clint Eastwood, John Wayne, Tom Mix, Roy Rogers, the Lone Ranger...

And still they carry us as Broncos and Pintos, Mustangs, Pacers, and Colts, and as the power hidden under the hood. Even driving across the lawn and the golf course, we're still riding horses.

But all this about horses is the easy part. This is symbolism and the history of the horse, but what of its mystery, the horse that asks to be relieved of carrying the hero on its back? What of the horse of the soul against whose neck a young boy can cry his loneliness and speak his secret wishes, the horse a young girl cur-ries and combs and loves with more devoted passion than any-body anywhere?

Have you cared for a horse? Had its saliva on your hands? Watched its colic, felt its patience when being shod, carried water on a January morning and heard its mouth suck it back? Have you ever had to put one down? Or, dreamt of a hurt horse?

Within the headstrong extraversion and noble courage that gal-lop across continents and centuries, marking the migrations of civilizations and their conquests and retreats, within that roman-tic impulse, lies the delicacy, something internal and so invisible that only dreams seem able to recall.

Rituals, called "the horse sacrifice," aim to release that invisibility within the heroism of the horse, marking a separation of horse from hero. These rituals are the hard part, and they amaze with their pathos.

For instance, when the Buddha took up the ascetic path, he dismissed his charioteer and had no further use for his horse, Kanthaka. This separation from his master broke the horse's heart and he died of grief. Thus did the Buddha do away with his no longer needed horse-power. Kanthaka is remembered in Buddhist statuary as a little horse figure of faithfulness near to the great seated Buddha, horse reduced to a minor potency in Buddhism's constellation of images.

The great Hindu horse-sacrifice (*asvamedha*) reaches back to the fourth millennium B.C.E. A conquering king would let a prize horse wander freely to graze accompanied by a band of young warriors. The territory covered by the horse became, as it were, the king's grazing grounds—the horse representing the limitless, libidinal energy of expansion. "When this stately animal...had wandered over the earth for the full cycle of a year, extending its adventurous stroll of conquest as far as it pleased and wherever it chose, it was then escorted home again to be slaughtered with the most elaborate and solemn rites" (Zimmer, *Philosophies of India*, 134).

Once the king was established, the expansionism that took him to the throne was no longer needed. The way of conquest is not the way of rule. One God or animal vehicle supports ambition, while another God or animal vehicle maintains what has been achieved. Thus, kings as kings are often presented as lions, elephants, bulls, eagles, that is, as supreme lords of consistency rather than as conquering heroes. By their steeds you can recognize their characters.

This brings us to Mars, God of battle-rage. You will have noticed that the horse in the Hindu story is accompanied by an honor guard of warriors. The Roman sacrifice of the October Horse makes this relation between horse and conquest even more explicit. Each year on October 15th on the field of Mars outside the city walls, a horse was killed by a javelin thrust to honor Mars. The scholar of early Italic religion, Dumezil, has collected the texts and explains the rites and their reasons. It was always a winning horse, for instance, the right-hand horse of a winning chariot. Why a "winning" horse? "Because Mars is the God appropriate to victory and strength." And, explains Plutarch, one "sacrifices to the Gods the things which they like and which have a connection with them," *eo ipso*, horses like Mars because horses are like unto Mars. Of course the Buddha had to let Kanthaka go; giving up the horse meant also giving up the martial way.

In dreams, too, horses are carefully slaughtered, sometimes flayed, put to death with a bullet, bled from the neck, buried in a pit. The dreamer is shocked, afraid for his or her own life, as if the death of the horse signaled the death of its own vitality, the forward carrying energy that is ready to get up and go into the day. Do these images of agony which the horse endures in dreams belong truly to the horse, or is it being sacrificed for its heroic master, the dreamer who cannot give up expansionist ambitions?

Alchemical psychology teaches the "horse sacrifice" much less literally. It makes use of the horse's belly, *venter equi* as an image of inward heat. Alchemy employs metaphors of fire for the intense concentration needed for soul-making. (In fact the alchemists were called "workers in fire.") The heat of the horse's belly referred to the digestion of events, brooding and incubating, instead of flaming up with martial temper. It is an inward heat, a contained fire.

Rather than slaying the horse or letting it go in order to be free of its force, alchemy suggests getting inside the horse, like Jonah in the whale. We interiorize and contemplate the urge to press forward, to run wild, to panic, to win. Instead of free-ranging conquest, you on top of the horse with reins of control in hand, you climb down and stay inside your animal drive, enveloped and cooked by its heat.

Alchemical psychology also uses an image of horse manure for this introverting heat. The closed glass vessel which holds the psychological stuff being "processed" may be kept warm at a steady temperature by burying it in horse dung. The steady heat refers to a slow and long focus on one's soul life. (*Focus*, by the way, is Latin for "hearth.") The glass vessel invites looking into and seeing through actions for their images. Stashing your soul stuff in a pile of manure means paying attention to the residues of your horse-driven urges and actions. You become conscious of the horse-shit component of your drivenness, the consequences of the life you have sped through and ridden over. As you stew in this fermentation, another kind of awareness begins to form.

From this perspective of the horse sacrifice and of getting inside the horse, rather than riding it heroically, we can look again at the story of the Trojan horse told in the *Odyssey* (Book VIII). You will recall that the Greeks were foiled again and again in their attempts to take Troy—until they built a great wooden horse which the Trojans, after much debate, took inside their impenetrable walls as a gift to honor the Gods. As we all know, the wooden horse was hollow and packed inside with the strongest of Greek heroes, who then rushed out of the horse's interior, sacked the city, and carried the day.

Yes, we all know the horse was hollow, but why didn't the Trojans suspect? Their imaginations were limited; they were still warriors; their horse had not been "sacrificed." The Greeks had taken the war to another level, from battle to the imagination of epic, from heroes to homecoming. After ten years of fighting, they got inside their own martial rage, their own need to conquer. They took Troy from the inside (not merely inside the walls literally), but metaphorically, imaginatively. They could imagine an end to the war—the hollow horse as artful image of that imaginative act. They entered its belly, as in alchemy.

So Troy fell, but fell to Homer. He conquered Troy with the Greek language, transforming battle into story, inventing in poetry what may or may not have happened in literal history. But for this to happen and culture to rise from the ruins of conquest, the horse had first to be hollowed.

FLOWERS AND FUNGI
ARCHETYPAL SEMIOTICS AND VISUAL METAPHOR

MICHAEL VANNOY ADAMS

J ungians express hardly any interest in semiotics, perhaps because Jung criticizes Freud as a semiotician. He says that for Freud the "symbol" is only a "sign," or a "symptom."[1] (Semiotics—from *semeion*—is the science of signs and signification.) It is curious that Jung never once cites Ferdinand de Saussure,[2] a fellow Swiss (not of Zürich but of Geneva) who is one of the two principal exponents of modern semiotics: Saussure in Europe and Charles Sanders Peirce in America. From the perspective of the general theory of semiotics that Saussure and Peirce establish, what Jung says about semiotics—and about Freud as a semiotician—is patently anachronistic and inadequate.

The psychoanalyst who emphasizes semiotics most is Jacques Lacan. Europeans like Roland Barthes tend to reduce semiotics to

---

1. *CW*, 8: 75 and 175.
2. Saussure, *Course in General Linguistics*, ed. Charles Bally and Albert Sechehaye, tr. Wade Baskin (New York: Philosophical Library, 1959).

Michael Vannoy Adams, D.Phil., C.S.W., is Senior Lecturer in Psychoanalytic Studies at the New School for Social Research, New York, where he is also a psychotherapist in private practice.

linguistics,[3] and Lacan is no exception to the rule. What interests him is the language of the unconscious. According to Lacan, if psychoanalysis is a talking cure, the individual is not so much a speaking subject as a subject spoken unconsciously by the system of linguistic signs that exist prior both to the individual and to any particular speech act. The linguistic sign is a unit that comprises a signifier (sound-image) and a signified (concept):

$$\text{Sign} \quad = \quad \frac{\text{Signifier}}{\text{Signified}} \quad = \quad \frac{\text{Sound-Image}}{\text{Concept}}$$

In this linguistic version of semiotics, the relation between signifier and signified is arbitrary or conventional. There is no natural connection between sound-image and concept, only a cultural one.[4]

A Jungian who attempts to engage Lacan and the Lacanians in a constructive exchange is Paul Kugler.[5] What interests Kugler is the possibility of an archetypal linguistics. The images that dominate psychoanalytic discourse, he emphasizes, are sound-images. For example, although dreams are experienced visually, they are recorded verbally and then reported orally. In addition, word as-

---

3. In *Elements of Semiology*, tr. Annette Lavers and Colin Smith (New York: Hill and Wang, 1968), Barthes says: "Saussure, followed in this by the main semiologists, thought that linguistics merely formed a part of the general science of signs. Now it is far from certain that in the social life of today there are to be found any extensive systems of signs outside human language" (9). He continues: "In fact, we must now face the possibility of inverting Saussure's declaration: linguistics is not a part of the general science of signs, even a privileged part, it is semiology which is a part of linguistics." According to Barthes, such an inversion, which subsumes semiotics (or semiology) within linguistics, elucidates "the unity of the research" that currently obtains in "psycho-analysis" and other disciplines "round the concept of signification" (11).
4. Lacan, "The Agency of the Letter in the Unconscious or Reason since Freud," *Ecrits: A Selection*, tr. Alan Sheridan (New York: W. W. Norton, 1977), 146-178.
5. Kugler, "Jacques Lacan: Postmodern Depth Psychology and the Birth of the Self-Reflexive Subject," in Polly Young-Eisendrath and James A. Hall (eds.), *The Book of the Self: Person, Pretext, and Process* (New York and London: New York UP, 1987), 173-184.

sociations provide the very basis of the dialogic process in the psychoanalytic session, which consists of talking and not just listening but really hearing—with the third ear. Kugler reflects that psychoanalytic theory has a relation, historically, to psycholinguistic research—in particular, to the experiments that Jung conducts on word associations and that establish the existence of the complex and, independently of Freud, confirm the function of repression. According to Kugler, perhaps the most important result of these experiments is the realization by Jung that the unconscious process by which word associations constitute a complex is essentially a phonetic affair. It is the way a word sounds—and resounds—that tends to determine the unconscious nexus of associations.[6]

As an example of this phonetic phenomenon, Kugler recounts a dream that Freud interpolates from another source. A woman has a dream of *"the centre of a table with flowers."* The analyst in this case confidently asserts that "the table with its floral centre-piece symbolized herself and her genitals." Among the flowers are violets. As an association to "violet," the woman offers "violate" (which surprises the analyst, to whom "viol," the French word for rape, occurs). This is the gloss that Freud quotes: "The dream had made use of the great chance similarity between the words *'violet'* and *'violate'*—the difference in their pronunciation lies merely in the different stress upon their final syllables—in order to express 'in the language of flowers' the dreamer's thoughts on the violence of defloration (another term that employs flower symbolism)."[7] In this case, the dream concerns virginity and the loss of it, and the linguistic sign has this particular structure:

Signifier(s)	Sound-Image(s)	Violet, Violate, Violent, etc.
Signified	Concept	Defloration

---

6. Kugler, *The Alchemy of Discourse: An Archetypal Approach to Language* (Lewisburg: Bucknell University Press, 1982), 14-18; Kugler, "Involuntary Poetics," *New Literary History: A Journal of Theory and Interpretation*, 15 (1983-84), 491-501.
7. *SE*, 5: 374-75.

Although the result is an apparently random—or arbitrary—homonymic effect, Kugler notes that, phonetically, the English language enables, even encourages the pun. Such an association of sound-images, he asserts, is a function of an archetypal fantasy—a defloration fantasy—that establishes, linguistically, an iconic (or metaphorical) connection between flowers and female genitals.

Kugler states that the basis of this relation is verbal (or phonetic) rather than visual:

> As to the metaphorical meaning, it would be a very poor explanation to state that flowers look like female genitals; therefore, they have been so called. We must admit that "flowers" and "female genitals" have very little in common on the level of object realities about which we are conscious, but if one looks into the archetypal implications of both ideas, one will discover a hidden association between "flowers" and the "violation" of "female genitals" in the evidence of language. In doing so we shall find first of all that one meaning, "violation," is related to another meaning, "flower," through an archetypal image, a syncretic fantasy, which imagistically connects both meanings. For this reason the sound pattern denoting "flower" does not stand alone; it is not an isolated phenomenon, but is connected by phonetic associations with other words. It belongs to a *complex of associations which all phonetically refer to the same archetypal fantasy.*[8]

Kugler privileges sound-images over sight-images. What is pertinent to Kugler is not whether flowers and female genitals look alike (he contends that objectively, on the level of physical reality, they have, in fact, very little in common as referents) but that "violet," "violate," "violent," etc., do sound alike and that this

8. Kugler, *The Alchemy of Discourse*, 19-21. In *Metaphor: A Psychoanalytic View* (Berkeley, Los Angeles, and London: University of California Press, 1978), Robert Rogers discusses not the violet, as Kugler does, but the rose. Rogers implicitly emphasizes sight-images (rather than sound-images) when he asserts that the metaphorical significances of the rose comprise that which is "phallic—if we include the thorns; and almost everything that pertains to genitality, including related material like defloration and the blood associated with that act" (128).

concatenation of signifiers, in psychical reality, has an archetypal basis in the fantasy of defloration as a signified.[9]

---

9. In *The Alchemy of Discourse*, Kugler also cites a carnation dream (18) that Theodore Thass-Thienemann recounts. In *Symbolic Behavior* (New York: Washington Square Press, 1968), Thass-Thienemann says: "A girl college student reported the following dream: She went with her boyfriend to the junior prom. The boyfriend brought her a *carnation*. She was very pleased and in high spirits. She wore a beautiful white evening dress. They entered the ballroom exuberantly. They went in together. They attracted everyone's attention but to her great embarrassment she first perceived some bloodstains on her white evening gown and soon found out the blood dripped from her carnation. The flowers were bleeding. She left the ballroom in great embarrassment. She awoke with palpitations." A plausible association might be to menstruation. "But why," Thass-Thienemann wonders, "did the blood drip from the carnation?" A more probable association, one that he presumes the dreamer has profoundly repressed, is defloration. "It is suggested," he says, "by the verbal form *de-flower* which might be connected in the mind of the dreamer with 'bleeding.'" As he interprets the dream, it "does not speak of menstruation anxiety but rather of a penetration anxiety which might be an attribute of self-conscious virginity." According to Thass-Thienemann, however, this meaning of the dream does not explain, specifically, the bleeding of a carnation: "The girl knew nothing of Latin, she was unaware of the fact that in Latin *carnis* means 'flesh.' She did not think even of *in-carnation*, 'becoming flesh,' and had no idea how this word *incarnation* could have anything to do with her 'carnation.' One may say in this case, not the carnation started to bleed but *vulnera recrudescunt*, an old scar started bleeding, an old forgotten meaning which did not exist in the conscious mind of the dreamer received some vitalizing energy from her unconscious, and became alive again in her dream. It is the case of the return of the repressed." In contrast to Kugler, who emphasizes the phonetic unconscious, Thass-Thienemann posits a phylogenetic or collective etymological unconscious: "While withdrawing from the perceptual daytime world and regressing to the state of the dream, this girl found an association which once was an actual idea in the mind of our prehistoric ancestry but has long been forgotten by the present generations" (179-180). As Kugler notes, this reliance on etymology is reductive in the extreme (31n.). In *The Individual and His Dreams* (New York: Signet, 1972), Calvin S. Hall and Vernon J. Nordby paraphrase the carnation dream that Thass-Thienemann mentions, as well as the interpretation that he proposes. They then add: "The reader may be interested in looking up the etymology of another flower name, the *orchid*, a flower which is given by a man to a woman as a token of affection" (138). Hall and Nordby imply that the word "orchid" has a sexual significance—and so it does. The etymological derivation is from *orchis*, Greek for testicle. This does not mean, however, as Hall and Nordby seem to suggest, that a corsage of orchids is a gift of testicles from a man to a woman, for it is not the flower but the root, the bulb not the blossom, that resembles the gland. *The Oxford Dictionary of English Etymology*, ed. C. T. Onions

These words share a morpheme that Kugler maintains is archetypal. I. A. Richards defines a morpheme as follows:

> Two or more words are said to share a morpheme when they have, at the same time, something in common in their meaning and something in common in their sound. The joint semantic-phonetic unit which distinguishes them is what is called a morpheme. It is the togetherness of a peculiar sound and a peculiar meaning for a number of words.
>
> Thus *flash, flare, flame, flicker, flimmer* have in common the sound (fl-) and a suggestion of a "moving light"—and this joint possession is the morpheme.... So with "smoothly wet" and (sl-) in *slime, slip, slush, slobber, slide, slither.*[10]

When Richards discusses the practical value of the term, he adds a note of caution:

> This pedantic looking term, *morpheme*, is useful because with its help we manage to avoid saying that the sound (sl-) somehow itself means something like "smoothly wet or slippery" and gain a way of saying no more than that a group of words which share that sound also share a peculiar meaning. And that is all we are entitled to say. To go further and say that the words share the meaning *because* they contain this sound and because this sound has that meaning is to bring in more than we do know. And actually it is a bad explanation. It is not the shared sound but each of the words which has the meaning.[11]

Thus in the fantasy of defloration it is not the sound ("viol-") that has the meaning. What constitutes a morpheme is several words, including in this case "violet," "violate," "violent," that together, as a group, share both a sound and a meaning. According to Richards, a morpheme has a semantic as well as a phonetic aspect. (Kugler also maintains that the phonetic similarity between "violet," "violate," and "violent" is "in accordance with the un-

---

(Oxford: Clarendon Press, 1966), states that the application of *orchis* is "to the shape of the tubers in most species" (631).
10. Richards, *The Philosophy of Rhetoric* (New York: Oxford UP, 1936), 59.
11. Richards, 59-60.

conscious associations of their semantic aspects." He elaborates as follows: "*Violate* means 'to rape'; *violent* implies a show of physical or emotional force; *violet* is a bluish-purplish flower."[12]

To attempt to explain the relation between flowers and female genitals as a function of a putative visual resemblance between referents, Kugler says, is to perpetrate a causalistic reduction of psychical reality to physical reality and, in the process, to commit the naturalistic fallacy.[13] This is apparently a variant of what Umberto Eco terms the referential fallacy, which he defines as the assumption that the meaning of the sign "has something to do with its corresponding object," or referent.[14] Psychoanalytically, the meaning may or may not. Neither Freud nor Jung believes that there is a necessary, deterministic connection between physical reality and psychical reality. There is absolutely no basis in psychoanalytic theory for the notion that physical reality is primary and constitutive while psychical reality is secondary and derivative. Quite to the contrary, in psychoanalytic ontology there is never a perception of a referent without a projection onto it. The meaning of "reality" is not given physically but is constructed psychically. The implication is that all images are "imagos"—that is, examples of the *psychical construction of reality*. Jung employs the term "imago" to emphasize the disparity, the inevitable and invariable incongruity, between the subject and the object, in relation to the imaginal, conceptual, and referential dimensions:

---

12. Kugler, *Alchemy of Discourse*, 23.
13. Kugler, *Ibid.*, 31n. In *Re-Visioning Psychology* (New York: Harper and Row, 1975), James Hillman provides this definition: "By the naturalistic fallacy, I mean the psychological habit of comparing fantasy events with similar events in nature. We tend to judge dream images to be right or wrong (positive or negative) largely by standards of naturalism. The more like nature an image appears, the more positive; the more distorted the image, the more negative. Rather like its sister fallacy in philosophy, the naturalistic fallacy in psychology also claims that the way it *is* in nature is the norm for how it *should* be in dreams." It also, according to Hillman, eventuates in the materialistic fallacy: "Naturalism soon declines into materialism, a view which regards the way things are in the perceptual world of things, facts and sense-realities to be the primary mode. It insists that material reality is first and psychic reality must conform with it: *psyche* must obey the laws of *physis* and imagination follow perception" (84).
14. Eco, *A Theory of Semiotics* (Bloomington and London: Indiana UP, 1976), 62.

Signifier	=	Image (Imago)	= Imaginal
Signified	=	Concept	= Conceptual
Object	=	Referent	= Referential

By means of an image, the subject may refer to an object, or concrete entity in physical reality, but the concept of that object in the psychical reality of the subject never corresponds accurately and exhaustively with the object. (Reference is not identical with correspondence, and in psychoanalytic epistemology the correspondence theory of truth is not applicable in a decisive or conclusive way.) Neither, as an "imago," is the image empirically determined by the object nor can it be logically reduced to the object.

According to Eco, meaning is not a natural category (that is, a function of the referent) but a cultural category. "Every attempt to establish what the referent of a sign is," he says, "forces us to define the referent in terms of an abstract entity which moreover is only a cultural convention."[15] For Eco, cultural conventions

---

15. Eco, *A Theory of Semiotics*, 66. In *The Alchemy of Discourse*, Kugler cites with approval Anthony Wilden, who interprets Saussure as saying that what is arbitrary is not the relation between signifier and signified (between sound-image and concept) but rather the relation between signifier and referent (102). In Jacques Lacan, *The Language of the Self: The Function of Language in Psychoanalysis*, ed. and tr. Wilden (Baltimore: Johns Hopkins UP, 1968), Wilden maintains that, for Saussure, "the arbitrariness lies between the signifier and 'reality'—that is, between the signifier and either 'real objects' or whatever is represented as reality by the social consensus of mutually shared presentations or referents." Wilden continues: "Thus, although Saussure speaks of the arbitrariness of the *signifier*, he really means what he says when he uses the expression 'the arbitrariness of the *sign*' as a synonym, for the linguistic sign *is* arbitrarily related to referents, which were probably conceived of by Saussure as 'real objects'" (216). If Eco is correct, however, in saying that it is cultural conventions (that is, cultural concepts) that define referents, then what is arbitrary is not only the relation between signifier and referent but also the relation between signifier and signified. For all practical purposes, the referent is, in effect, a concept—that is, a signified; or at least it proves impossible to define the referent except in terms of a signified. In short, the very definition of the referent is dependent on the way in which the subject conceives—or conceptualizes—the object. In *Nature and*

imply cultural codes, which provide the basis for systematic relations between signifier and signified (that is, between image and concept). For the sake of "theoretical purity," Eco says, an inquiry into codes requires that the referent be excluded from consideration. In this regard, the referent is a strictly extrinsic factor with a capacity to compromise the integrity of a theory of codes. Eco contrasts a theory of codes with a theory of truth-values. A theory of codes, he says, is concerned with intensional semantics (or connotation), while a theory of truth-values is concerned with extensional semantics (or denotation). The referent that is included in a theory of truth-values is not a concrete entity, actual object, or "token" but an abstract entity, "class" of actual or possible objects, or "type."[16] That is, the semantic extension, in this case, is not an object as such but a certain state of affairs that is more or less typical (as in archetype or stereotype).

In the context of the effort by Kugler to develop an archetypal linguistics, sound-images are obviously more germane than sight-images. What I advocate, however, is a more expansive perspective on images than sound-images alone afford. Rather than an archetypal linguistics, which would emphasize sound-images exclusively, I propose an archetypal semiotics—an *imagistics*—which would comprise sound-images, sight-images, taste-images, touch-images, and smell-images comprehensively.[17] An archetypal semi-

---

Language: A Semiotic Study of Cucurbits (London, Boston, and Henley: Routledge and Kegan Paul, 1980), Ralf Norrman and Jon Haarberg assert that metaphor constitutes an exception to this rule and therefore requires a serious consideration of the referent: "Relations between referents—that is, relations between, for example, physical objects—are sometimes thought to be outside the realm of linguistics"—not to mention the realm of semiotics. To the contrary, Norrman and Haarberg insist that "at least in the study of plant symbolism"— which, of course, comprises flower symbolism—"they cannot be ignored." Referents must be included. "As to the necessity of taking 'real-world relations' into account, metaphors, similes and figurative language are a special case," Normann and Haarberg declare, "because these signs are not arbitrary." At the very least such metaphors are not entirely arbitrary. The decisive issue, Normann and Haarberg emphasize, is "the degree of arbitrariness" (5-6).

16. Eco, *A Theory of Semiotics*, 60-61.

17. Michael Vannoy Adams, "Deconstructive Philosophy and Imaginal Psychology: Comparative Perspectives on Jacques Derrida and James Hillman," *Journal of Literary Criticism*, 2, 1 (June 1985), 23-39. Reprinted in Rajnath (ed.), *Decon-*

otics would acknowledge not just one but all five senses (sound, sight, taste, touch, and smell) as the media by means of which signification occurs—as follows:

Signifier(s) = Sound-, Sight-, Taste-, Touch-, and Smell-Image(s)
―――――――――――――――――――――――――――――――――――
Signified   = Concept
―――――――――――――――――
Object   = Referent

Inevitably, an archetypal semiotics would consider seriously the primacy of sight-images in the unconscious (and especially in the experience of dreams) and on that basis would, I believe, quite properly qualify a bias that tends to exaggerate the importance of sound-images.

One of the most important myths in contemporary psychoanalytic theory is a flower myth: the myth of Narcissus. It is a myth of death and rebirth. When Narcissus dies, he is reborn as a flower, the narcissus. The narcissus figures prominently in another myth, the myth of Persephone.[18] In the version that Carl Kerenyi recounts, Persephone is a maiden, playing with other maidens and "picking flowers—roses and crocuses, violets, irises and hyacinths." She also almost picks another flower, the narcissus, that Gaia, to please Hades, "had caused to spring up, a radiant wonder, as a wile to seduce the maiden." In semiotic terms, it is not a sound-image but a sight-image (as well as a smell-image) that is so seductive. According to Kerenyi, "All who beheld the flower, both gods and men, were astonished." What is seen is a flower with a "hundred blossoms" (what is smelled is a "sweet fragrance").[19] The implication is that narcissism entails susceptibility to seduction—in this case, to rape. In this regard, Patricia

struction: A Critique (London: Macmillan, 1989), 138-157, and in Richard P. Sugg (ed.), Jungian Literary Criticism (Evanston: Northwestern UP, 1992), 231-248.
18. Kugler also mentions this myth in The Alchemy of Discourse as an another example of "the defloration fantasy" (24-25).
19. Kerenyi, The Gods of the Greeks (London and New York: Thames and Hudson, 1951), 232.

Berry notes that "it is Persephone's narcissism (the flower Narcissus), in the Homeric tale, which brings Hades rushing up upon her."[20] It is precisely when Persephone reaches for the narcissus that Hades emerges from the underworld and carries her off. The myth of Persephone is a myth of the violent defloration of an inviolate, narcissistic, floral virginity, in which rape is a metaphor for an abrupt, drastic initiation from innocence into experience, from surface into depth, from world into underworld.[21]

---

20. Berry, *Echo's Subtle Body: Contributions to an Archetypal Psychology* (Dallas: Spring, 1982), 23.

21. In *The Therapeutic Experience and Its Setting: A Clinical Dialogue* (New York and London: Jason Aronson, 1980), Robert Langs and Leo Stone discuss the potentially seductive significance of flowers. Langs describes a patient who experienced "a seduction in her early adolescence by an older man, but not sexual intimacy, and other early seductions." This patient appeared for an early therapy session "carrying a bouquet of fall flowers." She presented the flowers as a gift to the therapist, who, not without some trepidation over the possibility that they "might well enhance erotic components of the transference," accepted them, in the belief that to reject them might well have had even worse therapeutic consequences (302-303). Stone argues that the decision either to accept or reject the flowers depends entirely on the context—on the significance, to the specific patient, of such a gift. According to Stone, the flowers might signify nothing at all sexual to the patient. Langs, however, says: "In my experience, in many, many instances when flowers have shown up unexpectedly, there has already been an unconscious countertransference problem in the analyst that has helped to create the conditions under which this occurs" (323). He continues: "To try briefly to define this: by accepting the flowers and accepting then this gift of love, he directly gratifies the pathological unconscious fantasies, and she must now respond to him as a participant, rather than as a nonparticipant.... In my opinion, his taking the flowers puts him in a compromised position, and the unconscious sexual gratification renders the patient vulnerable to further regression. We can postulate that she has within herself the residuals derived from experiences with seductive figures in her early relationships—her father—or there may have been a certain seductiveness in her mother and inappropriate interactions that helped to create her pathology. Now the analyst has behaved in a way that's in keeping with those earlier pathogenic figures, with the same loss of control and inappropriate seductiveness, and it's going to be very difficult for her to distinguish him from those earlier pathogenic figures" (324-325). In *The Symbolic Quest: Basic Concepts of Analytical Psychology* (New York: G. P. Putnam's Sons, 1969), Edward C. Whitmont mentions a dream in which the dreamer receives a bouquet of flowers from a female figure with whom he is in love. As Whitmont interprets the dream, the woman is a personification of the anima, an archetypal image of emergent emotion in the dreamer. From this perspective, the dreamer's flowers indicate that "his life will henceforth bloom." According to Whitmont,

Freud says, explicitly, that *"flowers* indicate women's genitals, or, in particular, virginity."[22] In the controversy over whether a

---

the dream implies that a conscious relation to the anima "may lead to the realm of 'flowers'"—that is, "to the source of creativity" (197-198).

22. *SE*, 15: 158. Freud also says that certain flowers indicate men's genitals, both penis and testicles, in combination. As an example, he includes "the tripartite lily—the so-called *fleur-de-lis*"—among what he calls "stylized versions of the male genitals" (164). In *Collected Papers on Schizophrenia and Related Subjects* (New York: International UP, 1965), Harold F. Searles recounts a flower dream that a woman patient, Edith, reported. She said: "'Dr Searles, you know I've told you that I very seldom dream. But I had a dream the night before last. You re- member that purse I have with flowers on the side of it? I dreamed that I rushed around so much that I lost the flowers from my purse, and I saw another woman pick them up and put them on *her* purse, and I said, [tone of strong protest] "She's taking *my* flowers!"'" Searles continues: "She then went on, with much interest, to contrast the feeling she had had in the dream, describing it now in the following way: a sharp intake of the breath, with 'I lost my flowers!'—to the feeling she had had a few weeks previously when, while downtown shopping, she had seen a woman with a purse almost like her own, except that the other woman's purse had flowers on the top, whereas Edith's purse had flowers on the side. Edith described her feeling on that earlier, real-life occasion with a tone of pleasure, 'She has almost the same as mine!' In saying how different from this had been the feeling in the dream, she said, 'I guess I do feel that something has been taken away from me.'" Searles does not interpret the flowers, much less the dream. He merely comments: "It did not become established in that hour what the 'something' might be, and I was left with this as an unanswered question in my own mind. In the earlier years of our work, she had very often indeed ex- pressed her conviction that she had been robbed; she had been unable for years to express a feeling of *loss* as such, but instead had felt deliberately robbed, of this or that person or thing, by maliciously inclined other persons, including myself" (703-704). If true to character, Freud would not have been reluctant to interpret the dream—sexually, of course. According to him, both purses (*SE*, 5: 373) and flowers are a typical symbol of the female genitals, and flowers, in par- ticular, are symbols of virginity. In all probability, Freud would have inter- preted the loss (or robbery) of flowers as a loss of virginity, a loss of innocence, a defloration. In *The Handbook of Dream Analysis* (New York: Liveright, 1951), Emil A. Gutheil presents the flower dream of another woman: "I am going up- hill—I do not know where. I hold a bunch of flowers in my hand, wrapped in white paper. I hold on to it very tightly. I know that someone wants to take it away from me. Suddenly, I feel a force coming from above, like a terrific wind, and the flowers are torn away from me. I stay there, like a dead person, un- happy, and cry." Gutheil interprets the dream as follows: "The flowers represent her craving for a pure and innocent love. She has dissociated love from sex. She could indulge in the latter without violating the former. The 'someone' who wants to take away her vow of chastity is the man. The man (also the analyst)

picture is worth more than a word, a sight-image more than a sound-image, Freud values the visual in this case. Contrary to the position that Kugler articulates, Freud apparently believes that, objectively, flowers and female genitals have much in common—by nature rather than by culture: that is, as referents in physical reality. Evidently, they have enough in common to facilitate the construction, in psychical reality, of a visual metaphor.

Kugler is not the only individual ever to question this tenet of Freudian theory. For example, one critic of psychoanalysis, in an extremely sarcastic tone, ridicules the interpretation of flowers in a dream by Freud. Andrew Salter maintains that he could plausibly interpret not only the flowers but also the water and rocks in the dream "as the female genitals, and I could also—but no. I think this is quite enough." Salter declares that "Freud's dreams, in fact, *anyone's dreams*, can receive an almost infinite series of psychoanalytic interpretations"—none of them, on the basis of the available evidence, with any more validity or veridicality than the others.[23] Consistent with this version of psychoanalytic

---

deprives her of her childhood dreams of chastity" (403). In *Dream Analysis: A Practical Handbook for Psycho-analysts* (New York: Brunner/Mazel, 1978), Ella Freeman Sharpe recounts two dreams in which flowers are, respectively, picked and planted. Sharpe regards these dreams as psychical responses of the dreamers to physical experiences. She infers that in the first dream the image of picking flowers is a metaphorical allusion to masturbation (86). Evidently, this is another example of the symbolic equation of flowers with female genitals. (Presumably, the dreamer is a woman, although Sharpe does not say so.) The image of planting flowers occurs in the final dream of a woman eighty-one years of age just three days before she died of a persistent disease: "I saw all my sicknesses gathered together and as I looked they were no longer sicknesses but roses and I knew the roses would be planted and that they would grow." Sharpe interprets the dream as a poignant expression of the hope that sustained the woman in life and consoled her in death. "It is Eros alone," Sharpe says, "who *knows* that the roses will be planted and will grow" (200-201). In this second dream of flowers, eros is not (literally) sex but (metaphorically) life. In *On Dreams and Death: A Jungian Interpretation*, trans. Emmanuel Xipolitas Kennedy and Vernon Brooks (Boston and London: Shambhala, 1986), Marie-Louise von Franz interprets the flower as a symbol of the self, or soul. According to von Franz, dreaming of flowers as the dreamer is dying symbolizes "the post-mortal existence of the soul" (35). In this case, resurrection is refloration.

23. Salter, *The Case against Psychoanalysis* (New York: Henry Holt, 1952), 77-81.

events, Paul Roazen recounts an anecdote by Helene Deutsch from the Vienna Psychoanalytic Society:

> Helene once remarked that at the first meeting of the society she attended, Isidor Sadger gave a paper on flowers in dreams; he had gone overboard in emphasizing the sexual themes that Freud had introduced, and Sadger interpreted flowers as genital symbols. At the time Helene wondered to herself whether flowers could not also be just flowers. Among his Viennese adherents Freud put up with people he was dubious about: Sadger, for instance, had an almost pornographic interest in sex.[24]

Sometimes, evidently, a flower is only a flower.

Similarly, Georgia O'Keeffe adamantly maintains that the flowers she paints are in no sense symbolic. Laurie Lisle, however, says of O'Keeffe's flowers that in spite of "her best efforts to be realistic and defuse the Freudian talk, her trembling, feathery, unfurling petals reminded people of genitalia just as the abstractions had done." According to Lisle, in effect if not intent, the paintings provoke individuals to visualize imaginally the sexual organs of both men and women: "Large, engorged stamens and corollas suggested male genitals, while dark recesses ('soft, enormous caves,' said *Time* in 1928) that invited penetration strongly suggested female vulvas." To the chagrin of at least one patron of the arts, O'Keeffe is even an inadvertent advocate of sex education. "One woman who owned a big O'Keeffe flower painting was shocked to discover someone teaching a child the facts of life from it," Lisle says. "When she hastily rehung it in her bedroom, a friend remarked, 'Oh, I'm so glad you moved that vagina out of the living room.'" Lisle notes that, against any imputation that the flowers she paints are sexually symbolic, O'Keeffe protests that the experience of female artists is not restricted to any single aspect of existence and also observes that when male artists such as Marsden Hartley and Charles Demuth "painted flowers, theirs were not interpreted erotically." According to O'Keeffe, a sexual

---

24. Roazen, *Helene Deutsch: A Psychoanalyst's Life* (Garden City: Doubleday Anchor, 1985), 150.

interpretation is a subjective (and perhaps also a sexist) projection. Thus she writes in an exhibition catalog that any sexual connotation is only in the eye of the beholder, who associates all too freely to flowers:

> Well—I made you take time to look at what I saw and when you took time to really notice my flower you hung all your own associations with flowers on my flower and you write about my flower as if I think and see what you think and see of the flower—and I don't.

It is not the flowers that are suggestive; it is the individual who is suggestible.[25] At least that is the position of O'Keeffe, who, like Gertrude Stein, insists that a flower is a flower is a flower. (Or, as Joseph Campbell says: "What—I ask—is the meaning of a flower? And having no meaning, should the flower, then, not be?"[26])

Another woman artist, however, who mentions O'Keeffe as an important precursor, paints explicitly symbolic flowers to serve a feminist purpose. In 1972, in an effort at liberation from "the limits of the female role," Judy Chicago begins to explore the spatial possibilities of interiority in an effort to establish a distinctively feminine perspective:

> I used the flower as the symbol of femininity, as O'Keeffe had done. But in my images the petals of the flowers are parting to reveal an inviting but undefined space, the space beyond the confines of our own femininity. These works symbolized my longing for transcendence and personal growth. They were my first steps in being able to make clear, abstract images of my point of view as a woman.

In the art of other women, Chicago discerns an intimate connection between female body and "central image" (frequently a flower), between skin and canvas (Chicago says, almost like a mystic: "I was the painting and the painting was me"), and specu-

---

25. Lisle, *Portrait of an Artist: A Biography of Georgia O'Keeffe* (New York: Seaview, 1980), 138-139.
26. Campbell, *The Flight of the Wild Gander: Explorations in the Mythological Dimension* (New York: Viking, 1969), 188.

lates that O'Keeffe experiences "a similar connection between herself and her work." Of O'Keeffe, Chicago says: "In her paintings, the flower suggests her own femininity, through which the mysteries of life could be revealed." Eventually, Chicago produces a thematic series of lithographs, "Through the Flower," as well as a book by that title. With Miriam ("Mimi") Schapiro, she conducts a survey of art, much of it floral, by other women:

> Then Mimi and I looked at work together, examining paintings and sculptures of women known and unknown, concentrating on those who had worked abstractly. From our experiences as artists, we both had an understanding of how to look for the hidden content in women's work. What we discovered in our studies and later, in our studio visits overwhelmed me; and reinforced my own early perceptions. We found a frequent use of the central image, often a flower, or abstracted flower form, sometimes surrounded by folds or undulations, as in the structure of the vagina. We saw an abundance of sexual forms—breasts, buttocks, female organs. We felt sure that what we were seeing was a reflection of each woman's need to explore her own identity, to assert her sense of her own sexuality, as we had both done.

In an article on female imagery in art, Chicago and Schapiro caution against a reductive interpretation of the symbolically sexual. It should not, they say, be regarded "in a simplistic sense as 'vaginal art.'" Such an attitude simply perpetuates a stereotype. In comparison, Chicago and Schapiro note that "women artists have used the central cavity which defines them as women as the framework for the complete reversal of the way in which women are seen in the culture." These women artists employ the central image in an assertive effort radically to alter perception (or preconception):

> That is: to be a woman is to be an object of contempt and the vagina, stamp of femaleness, is despised. The woman artist, seeing herself as loathed, takes that very mark of her otherness and by asserting it as the hallmark of her iconography, establishes a vehicle by which to state the truth and beauty of her identity. The image in the center is content in form; in this sense, the

flower as a female genital serves, Chicago says, as "a metaphor for the female self," and physical reality, by means of an icon, acts as the medium of expression for psychical reality.[27]

It is not only female artists but also male scientists who depict flowers as symbolically sexual—and in a style evidently evocative of O'Keeffe. Stanley Edgar Hyman is unsure of the extent to which Charles Darwin is conscious of the graphic, even porno-graphic quality of certain illustrations in the books he publishes, but when Darwin discusses the fertilization of flowers and the propagation of plants, he does so with the express intent not to offend the sensibilties of women readers. Darwin describes, as an evolutionary naturalist, orchids and insectivorous plants in par-ticular. Hyman comments that many of the images of orchids are "phallic: tendrils climbing, shoots circumambulating warily, roots forcing and penetrating, pollinia erecting and depressing." Impres-sive as this male imagery may be, it is not what interests Hyman most:

> Much more dramatically, however, both orchids and insec-tivorous plants are female imagery, vulvar, vaginal: attracting, clutching, catching the probosces of insects, enslaving in their service or mercilessly destroying. The illustrations in the *Orchid* book are more lurid than Georgia O'Keeffe's flower paintings, and the illustrations in *Insectivorous Plants* of Darwin's beloved *Drosera* or the American *Dionaea*, the Venus Fly-trap, are the witchcraft fantasy or nightmare of *vagina dentata*.

Hyman concludes that in Darwin the exotic is, symbolically, the erotic.[28] The question remains, however, whether the metaphor is in nature or in culture. For example, is the interpretation in this case merely another anthropomorphic, perversely vulgar projec-tion of vulvar and vaginal associations onto floral illustrations that predictably imply, to Hyman (who is, after all, not a woman but a man—and a twentieth-century man under the influence of

27. Chicago, *Through the Flower: My Struggle as a Woman Artist* (Garden City: Doubleday Anchor, 1977), 141-144.
28. Hyman, *The Tangled Bank: Darwin, Marx, Frazer and Freud as Imaginative Writers* (New York: Athenuem, 1962), 73-74.

Freud), a motif of emasculation? Is this metaphor a discovery, or
is it an invention (or convention)? Does Hyman (or Darwin) find
it out from nature, or does he make it up or take it up from culture? Is it fact or artifact? Is it archetype or stereotype?

   In regard to the sexually symbolic, Claudette Sartiliot observes
that flowers by nature—that is, by "actual morphology"—seem to
have an iconic effect. She notes that "the receptacle-shaped corolla
readily becomes a symbol of the womb, whereas the pistil with its
erect stylus points to phallic symbolism."[29] Jonathan Sturrock,
however, asserts in no uncertain terms: "Flowers have no *natural*
significance, only a cultural or conventional one."[30] This is the
position of the twentieth-century structuralist; it is the very opposite of the opinion of the nineteenth-century transcendentalist.
For instance, Henry David Thoreau, like Freud, believes that
flowers are symbols of virginity—and naturally so. Thoreau contends that the connection is necessary and not culturally contingent. To the transcendentalist, nature is not only nature. A flower
is not only a flower; it is a sight-image, a signifier with a transcendental signified: in this case, the concept of virginity, or chastity.
In contrast to chastity, Thoreau says, sensuality causes language
to lose "many pregnant symbols." The language of flowers, he
elaborates, comprises figures of speech that pose various moral
alternatives:

> Flowers, which, by their infinite hues and fragrance cele-
> brate the marriage of the plants are intended for a symbol of the
> open and unsuspected beauty of all true marriage, when man's
> flowering season arrives.
>   Virginity too is a budding flower, and by an impure mar-
> riage the virgin is deflowered. Whoever loves flowers, loves vir-
> gins and chastity. Love and lust are as far asunder as a flower
> garden is from a brothel.[31]

29. "Herbarium, Verbarium: The Discourse of Flowers," *Diacritics*, 18, 4
(Winter 1988), 72.
30. Sturrock, "Introduction," in *Structuralism and Since: From Levi-Strauss to
Derrida* (Oxford: Oxford UP, 1979), 7.
31. Thoreau, *Early Essays and Miscellanies, The Writings*, ed. Joseph J. Molden-
hauer et al. (Princeton: Princeton UP, 1975), 276.

As Thoreau describes them, flowers are one of those particular natural facts that Ralph Waldo Emerson says are symbols of particular spiritual facts (just as nature is the symbol of spirit).[32] In this regard, nature, traditional personification of the female and the feminine, is by no means prudish; what she conceals she also reveals. "Nothing is too pointed, too personal, too immodest, for her to blazon," Thoreau observes. "The relations of sex, transferred to flowers, become the study of ladies in the drawing-room." Apparently, nature uses flowers to symbolize the female genitals and fungi to symbolize the male genitals: "While men wear fig leaves, she grows the *Phallus impudicus* and *P. caninus* and other phallus-like fungi."[33] Freud notices the same impudently pudendal phenomenon: "The mushroom is an undoubted penis-symbol: there are mushrooms [fungi] which owe their sytematic name (*Phallus impudicus*) to their unmistakable resemblance to the male organ."[34] In practice—that is, in nature—Thoreau confirms transcendentalist theory. Thus he discovers "an enormous toadstool, or fungus, a sharply conical parasol." Not only the shape but also the size is an issue for Thoreau, who evidently employs the comparative method. "The whole height," he remarks, "was sixteen inches." As a measure of the masculine and a comment on it, the fungus conveys a potent implication. "It suggests a vegetative force," Thoreau says, "which may almost make man tremble for his dominion."[35]

A flower, however, may also resemble the union of male and female genitals in sexual intercourse. At least that is what Robert

32. Emerson, *Nature* (1836), *Collected Works*, ed. Robert E. Spiller and Alfred R. Ferguson (Cambridge, Mass.: Belknap Press of Harvard UP, 1971), 1: 17-23.
33. Thoreau, *The Journal*, ed. Bradford Torrey and Francis Allen (Boston: Houghton Mifflin, 1949), 3: 255.
34. *SE*, 15: 164. Freud mentions a girl "who was afraid to pick a flower or even to pull up a mushroom, because it was against the command of God, who did not wish living seeds to be destroyed." According to him, this fear "arose from a memory of religious maxims of her mother's directed against precautions during coitus, because they mean that living seeds are destroyed" (*SE*, 1: 249). Freud also employs the mushroom as a metaphor for the ultimate unknowability of every dream. He says that "the spot where it reaches down into the unknown" is comparable to the mycelium from which a mushroom emerges (*SE*, 5: 525).
35. Thoreau, *The Journal*, 5: 270, 271.

Beverley observes and then describes in early eighteenth-century Virginia:

> About two years ago, walking out to take the Air, I found a little without my Pasture Fence, a Flower as big as a Tulip, and upon a Stalk resembling the Stalk of a Tulip. The Flower was of a Flesh Colour, having a Down upon one End, while the other was plain. The Form of it resembled the *Pudenda* of a Man and Woman lovingly join'd in one. Not long after I had discover'd this Rarity, and while it was still in Bloom, I drew a grave Gentleman, about an Hundred Yards, out of his Way, to see this Curiosity, not telling him any thing more, than that it was a Rarity, and such, perhaps, as he had never seen, nor heard of. When we arrived at the Place, I gather'd one of them, and put it into his Hand, which he had no sooner cast his Eye upon, but he threw it away with Indignation, as being asham'd of this Waggery of Nature. It was impossible to perswade him to touch it again, or so much as to squint towards so immodest a Representation. Neither would I presume to mention such an Indecency, but that I thought it unpardonable, to omit a Production so extraordinary.[36]

This specific flower is a peculiarity that affords Beverley a perfect opportunity for a practical joke. It is a sight-image that enables him to embarrass a very serious companion, an individual who never suspects that nature (in evident contrast to culture) serves such singularly obscene purposes.

More recently, it is a photographer rather than a painter who portrays flowers in a style that is quite sexually explicit. Lawrence Biemiller comments on the reputation of Robert Mapplethorpe among contemporaries: "In part because his photographs of nudes were unprecedented in their frankness, and in part because his technical skills allowed him to create unusually beautiful images—particularly of flowers—Mr. Mapplethorpe became one of the best-known photographers of his time." According to Biemiller, these flowers are perhaps more provocative even than certain

---

36. Beverley, *The History and Present State of Virginia* [1705], ed. Louis B. Wright (Charlottesville: Dominion Books, 1968), 140.

male nudes (some homoerotic, others sadomasochistic) that, in whole or part, involve Mapplethorpe in so much notoriety:

> Indeed, some of the exhibition's viewers find Mr. Mapplethorpe's flower images more graphic than his nudes—even those in which two people are posed to suggest a particular act or relationship. The interplay of shape and shadow in a 1984 close-up of a calla lily, for instance, emphasizes its curvaceousness and the texture of its surface to an extent that makes it unarguably sexual.[37]

In this case, similitude in nature (the resemblance between flower and genital, or other organ, at the level of physical reality) and extreme mastery of the photographic medium (the sheer aesthetic quality of the visual image) permit Mapplethorpe to achieve in art a verisimilitude evocative of sexuality at the level of psychical reality—that is, at the level of the metaphorical rather than the merely literal.

It is irrelevant whether or not the artist intends visibly to assert a natural connection between flower and female genital (O'Keeffe insists that she does not; Chicago declares that she does). What art means is not reducible to what artists intend. What is decisive is not the intention of the artist but rather the perceptions and—as a necessary concomitant—the projections of individuals. As Peirce defines the sign, it is something that signifies something to someone in some respect or another. For the realist and literalist, a flower is a flower is a flower—and only a flower. For the imagist and metaphorist, a flower may also be a female or male genital. In a sense, visual significance is always in the eye of the beholder. Someone must visually behold a significance in something in some respect. The eye of the beholder, however, is not only the mind's eye but also the body's eye, and just as there must always be a beholder, there must also always—except in hallucinations (or in pure figments of imagination)—a beheld, a referent. Just because not everyone will always behold the same visual significance in the beheld does not entail that significance is wholly sub-

---

37. Biemiller, "Behind the Debate over Mapplethorpe's Photographs," *Chronicle of Higher Education* (12 July 1989), B4.

jective or cultural. It is also almost always at least partly objective or natural.

In this regard, the verbal and visual dimensions are qualitatively different semiotically. Hearing with the third ear is different from seeing with the third eye. The resemblance between a sound-image that sounds like another sound-image is different not merely in degree but in kind from the resemblance between a sight-image that looks like another sight-image. Likeness in sound (say, between "violet," "violate," and "violent") is arbitrary (or conventional). Such phonetic or homonymic likeness is a random effect, an accident of linguistic history (except, perhaps, to a certain extent in the case of etymological derivations), however conveniently such associations may serve an individual as the basis for an unconscious complex—for example, a fantasy of defloration. That is, likeness in sound is not based on an objective similarity between referents. The *objects* violet, violation, and violence have nothing in common; only the *sound-images* "violet," "violation," and "violence" have something in common—the sound "viol-." In contrast, likeness in sight (say, between flowers and vaginas or between fungi and penises) is not strictly arbitrary. The referents of these sight-images are, in one respect or another, objectively similar (however little, as Kugler says, they may have in common on the level of object realities).

A verbal pun is a very special case of metaphor, one that depends for effect entirely on a similarity (or identity) of sounds ("violet," "violate," "violent")—and a *dissimilarity* of meanings. Phonetically, the sound-images are similar (or identical), but, semantically, the concepts are dissimilar. This is why, in fact, a verbal pun may seem "funny." In addition—and this is what I would emphasize—a verbal pun does not depend on any similarity (or any connection at all) between referents, or objects. Reference is utterly irrelevant to the formation of a verbal pun. For this reason, it would be erroneous to attempt to formulate a general theory of metaphor on the example of the verbal pun, for other kinds of metaphor—especially visual metaphor (or the visual pun)—may depend, to a considerable extent, on a similarity between referents.

The prejudice that attempts to reduce semiotics to linguistics uncritically privileges sound-images over sight-images, taste-images, touch-images, and smell-images, emphasizes the verbal dimension to the virtual exclusion of the visual and other dimensions, and, on that basis, indiscriminately insists that all signifiers (images) have an arbitrary relation not only to signifieds (concepts) but also to referents (objects). To the extent that psychoanalysis purports to be both a talking and a listening cure, it, too, has a linguistic, or verbal, bias—in spite of the fact that Freud describes the unconscious, especially in dreams, as fundamentally a visual dimension in which sight-images predominate. He says that dreams "think predominantly in visual images—but not exclusively."[38] According to Freud, the unconscious (or primary process) consists of thing-presentations (sight-images), while the conscious (or secondary process) consists of thing-presentations in conjunction with word-presentations (sound-images). He says that "the conscious presentation comprises the presentation of the thing plus the presentation of the word belonging to it, while the unconscious presentation is the presentation of the thing alone."[39] Freud does not (as Jung does with the technique of active imagination) recommend an experiential revisualization of the dream. He advocates an interpretative verbalization of it. Such interpretations are not arbitrarily contrived, he maintains, since dreams are, according to him, psychically determined, and symbols are conventionally defined—"generally known and laid down by firmly established linguistic usage."[40] In contrast to some semioticians, Freud thus acknowledges an important distinction between the arbitrary and the conventional. To the extent that he emphasizes linguistic usage, however, he tends to privilege the verbal over the visual dimension.

An exception that Freud allows to this rule is the case of certain symbols that are "comparisons"—by which he evidently means metaphors (in the sense of elliptical similes). Thus he mentions "comparisons between different objects which result in its being possible for one of them to be regularly put in the place of the

---

38. *SE*, 4: 49.
39. *SE*, 14: 201.
40. *SE*, 5: 342.

other." According to Freud, such comparisons are not arbitrary or conventional. "These comparisons," he maintains, "are not freshly made on each occasion; they lie ready to hand and are complete, once and for all." Nor are they exclusively the result of linguistic usage. They are universally available, at the general disposal of every individual. "This is implied," Freud says, "by their agreeing in the case of different individuals—possibly, indeed, in spite of differences of language." He concludes: "Linguistic usage covers only a small part of them."[41] Apparently, the basis of comparison is, in large part, nonlinguistic, or nonverbal—a function of visual similarity between objects, or referents.

The decisive difference between visual signifiers and verbal signifiers is that sight-images are both cultural *and* natural. They have not only a *contingent* (arbitrary and conventional) connection to signifieds (concepts) but also a *necessary* connection, in one respect or another, to objects (referents). In spite of what Eco says, a sight-image does have something to do with the object. The psychical construction of a visual metaphor entails an appreciation of a potential affinity simultaneously intrinsic to the referents of both sight-images, in conjunction. A visual metaphor *does not derive from* these referents (to adopt that position would be to commit the naturalistic fallacy), but the referents *do participate in and contribute to* the formation of the visual metaphor (to believe otherwise would be to prefer a subjectivistic attitude tantamount, at the extreme, to a solipsistic conceit, oblivious or indifferent to objects in external reality). The referents present an occasion or an opportunity (or even a convenient excuse) for the construction of a metaphor. That is, they are visually evocative (even provocative). They invite (or something about them invites) a metaphorical construction. The individual who psychically constructs a visual metaphor (like the practical joke that Beverley performs) sees through literal appearances to a metaphorical reality, which he may then attempt to persuade other individuals to see as he does. The visual metaphor may be either trite or novel, and the reaction of other individuals may be either tedium or surprise (or even, as Beverley says, indignation at an indecency).

---

41. *SE*, 15: 165-166.

An archetypal semiotics would be much more than a linguistics that privileges sound-images over sight-images. It would include all kinds of images and subtly discriminate between the metaphorical capacities of the different kinds (perhaps especially in relation to the controversy over how referents may participate in and what, if anything, they may contribute to the psychical construction of metaphors). Such a semiotics would, it seems to me, be particularly important to psychoanalysis, which exhibits a linguistic, or verbal, bias that tends, in effect, to be iconoclastic toward the iconic—and, in general, both unempathic and unsympathetic to the visual dimension, the sight-images that predominate in the unconscious.

In physical reality, flowers and fungi are not literally genital organs. In psychical reality, however, flowers may be vaginas, and fungi may be penises—metaphorically, or iconically—because these objects do, in fact, look alike, in some respect, to someone. That is, if individuals are suggestible, certain objects are suggestive, sometimes sexually so. (Nature, as Beverley says, is sometimes a wag.) Sometimes a flower is a vagina, sometimes a fungus is a penis.

IS MAGIC STILL ALIVE?

MORDECHAI SHUGAR

> . . . one person whose life will have been momentarily enhanced or forever changed by the magic of the image moving out of light into darkness.
>
> —John Griffin, *The Montreal Gazette*, Sept. 2, 1995.

Although this phrase came from a critic reviewing the recent Montreal World Film Festival, it might well have served to describe the latest Myth and Theatre Festival that took place in Avignon, France this past August (1995). The subject was Magic. The setting was religious: the old charterhouse of the 14th century monks at Villeneuve-lez-Avignon. The countryside was magnificent Provence, with its romantic charm visible and tasteable at every turn.

I brought some questions with me after a whirlwind two week tour through eastern Europe. Is magic still alive? Can it be conjured during a set time frame? Does it have anything to do with faith and ritual and myth for our own times?

It should be said at the outset that one of the old masters of the Jungian game, Rafael Lopez-Pedraza, author of *Hermes and His Children*, declined to attend, saying that this was too big a moun-

Mordechai (Murray) Shugar has worked for over 20 years as a taxi driver in Montreal, Quebec, Canada, where he is a regular contributor to the Newsletter of the C. G. Jung Society of Montreal, in whose October 1995 issue this article first appeared. He was a rewriter on the MythologICON project, a CD-ROM on Greek Mythology, created by Ginette Paris and a team at the University of Quebec in Montreal. He is currently organizing a joint venture between the French and English Jung Societies of Montreal to duscuss the issue of Quebec nationalism in a mutual context.

tain for him to climb. Perhaps he set the tone for the festival: many other invitees failed to materialize due to a host of last minute illnesses. One could not help but ask, from an archetypal perspective, were the gods themselves conspiring to make matters difficult?!

Another sign that the magic presented might not be what we had imagined occurred early on. In an introductory session, one of the stars of a previous festival told of the small miracle that had happened the last time. When a terrible rainstorm had threatened to cancel her outdoor dance performance, she sought an audience with Pope Innocent VI, whose remains are interred on the site of the monastery, pleading with him to let the show go on. Sure enough, the weather lifted and she did her wondrous performance: the very large black woman appeared to take flight in her ecstatic trance dance.

Well, here she was encouraging us to believe in the power of magic, faith, positive thinking or, (pagans forfend!) the power of dead Popes, when a dog that had wandered into the theatre nearly stole the show from her; all of her commands to him to leave at once were simply ignored! Were we in the presence of a force stronger than good intentions and magic itself? Had Coyote stolen aboard our flight and disembarked in southern France to accompany us and cause havoc?

True enough, certain *éminences grises* of the psychological world were absent. James Hillman and Charles Boer, founding Fathers of the Festival from its inception ten years ago, had also passed on the invitation. There had been rumours that the split between the worlds of psychology and art had been made complete. The children were now running their own show without the help of their forebears. I was inclined to look at it in the way Nor Hall had presented her Scenes from Therapy at the Notre Dame Festival of Archetypal Psychology in the summer of 1992 and again in Montreal in May of 1994: the psychological view of the world needed a different perspective, perhaps that of the dramaturge, a third party, who could see the dynamic between the therapist and the client; perhaps a god or a spirit at play, at work, at pains, in joy, at discovering a moment, a movement so subtle it could so easily escape detection if not for the finely tuned senses of the witness who catches and names the moment when magic is conjured. Nor would call her workshop at the festival "Magical Catches."

My partner and I were wandering through the grounds the first day in Villeneuve, newcomers to the place. After seeing the well in the middle of the courtyard of La Chartreuse, and taking a drink, we meandered around until we came upon our favorite diviner looking out from the second floor window of her cloister. She informed us that Joan of Arc had stopped at this place, at this spring, on her mission for God and country. We felt humbled that we were in such a presence. Would soul be saved, would bodies be burned, would there be lives at stake during our fortnight here? Given that activities began on August 6th, the fiftieth anniversary of Hiroshima, would that awful dark spirit of the world be visited upon us in such pleasant surroundings?

The format was ambitious and comprehensive. There were early morning warm-up exercises, voice workshops like "Polyphonic Singing," ritual sessions called "Between the Worlds," "African Dance," and master classes under the rubric "Unidentified Flying Subjects." Afternoons were given over to lectures. Among the subjects were a series of lectures by one of *Spring*'s best writers, Sonu Shamdasani, on the history of Psychoanalysis, or how to hammer the last nails into the coffin of Psychoanalysis. Jay Livernois, always provocative, took on the political Jesus, Casanova and the Occult, and towards the end of the festival, the perversities of Puritanism. He seemed determined to retrieve the ever dangerous Eros that had created a stir at the last festival on Aphrodite. Anthropologist Yves Lorelle spoke with great affection of the animalization of the hunter. The magician Paolo Lagazzi spoke and gave a demonstration of prestidigitation and its relation to writing. Rachel Pollack gave Tarot a judicious and imaginative look. Stephen Karcher presented his newly minted *I Ching*. Franc Chamberlain spoke of the magic influences in the theatre. All the worlds of magic that surround 20th century psychoanalysis were presented to put some perspective on the brainchild of Freud and Jung to see if it could pass scrutiny.

Evenings were devoted to videos of shamanic practices around the world, from voudun ceremonies in Haiti to flesh-piercing

rituals in the Philippines. There were also theatre and dance per-
formances, Siberian folk-rock music, new wave British poet-rock,
a full moon ceremony, even a human-sculpted Dionysian Mystery scene.

In a matter of days, it became apparent that one was easily over-
loaded on intellectual stimulation and the magic faded as the mind
spun.

The afternoons were also intended to give people opportunities
to meet again with the lecturers of the previous day or perform-
ers of the previous evening for further discussion. These sessions
were fetchingly called the "Medicine Tent." It was often a pleasure
to meet the people who had dedicated their lives to such art forms
as, say, the voice work of Jonathan Hart Makwaia; or to see the
sketches Yves Lorelle had made of the hunting drawings of the
Nigerian shamans.

It was also a chance to challenge the difficult and seemingly in-
accessible theatre piece called "The Angels' Hideout" which had
been created expressly for the festival. If the initial reaction in
many quarters had been misunderstanding and even disgust, at
least the explanation for the motivation behind the piece gave it
some redeeming quality. It proved to make more sense by the
time the festival had come to an end a week later, and the world
had come crashing in at the gates of paradise, with the news that a
second bomb had exploded in Paris, reminding one of the participants of a friend maimed by the previous round of terrorism
ten years ago. The lost and wounded souls and angels of the
world portrayed on the stage had their place even in such a sacred
retreat. Art and politics and psyche were not such remote rela-
tives. Hillman would have been pleased.

A brief word should be said about the Roy Hart Theatre which
is the artistic root of Pantheatre, whose members are the creative
genius of the Festival. We had met Enrique Pardo, the director of
Pantheatre, for the first time at the infamous Notre Dame Festival
and were inspired by even the briefest work with him. Something
about how his mercurial spirit enters his work moved me. It may
be a standard device in dance or theatre or voice training, for
which the Roy Hart is best known, but I know so little of it.
There is something in the exercises that stretches the individual

far beyond his usual boundaries of self-knowledge that tempted me to explore the work further. And we came to see every morning that ensemble work in the space moves the subject beyond his original conception of text or movement or self.

A case in point: Eight or nine people are moving around the room, one of them speaking a text she has brought with her from Paris. The instructions are to follow a leader around the room following not too closely, or too literally, changing the movement and improvising around it, if possible. The leaders have been told to be cruel: don't make it easy for the persons behind you to follow you. A chorus has been set up in a far corner of the room to find sounds that might or might not accompany the feeling conveyed by the group which occupies most of the working space.

The participants are a mix of professional dancers, actors, singers, and playwrights; there are also psychologists, taxi drivers, Economics profs and statisticians. From a corner of the room, the mournful cast of the dancers is felt and translated into a wail. This continues as the movement sinks to the ground, as bodies fall together; the text is not heard but the feeling is plain enough. The pity holds for too long and a laugh issues from the corner; it gains strength. The woman standing against the wall in front of the crowd of mourners begins to convulse hearing the chorus that joins her in mocking the scene. From a contagious sorrow arises a volcanic eruption from below that shakes the room. The end of the piece is lost in vague and forgotten gestures. Only a brief exchange remains, like a fragment from a dream that we try to hold onto in vain.

In the discussion afterward, we learned that the first woman who seemed to be crying had not really shed tears even if a deep sadness had been felt in her gestures by the singers in the corner. The second woman who picked up the feeling from the first and seemed surely to be in pain, she too had been performing what seemed to be the feeling conveyed in the ensemble. But the striking moment was this: we found out that it was the laughter that struck the second mourner as it rose up from the ground through her feet and coursed through her body. It was only then she felt the anguish of someone who is suffering and not only has no one's attention but is being mocked. There her suffering had truly come to life.

Like a theatre critic describing the play he has seen the previous night, this brief catch can do little to bring home the impact of what happens in the process of creating theatre. And even "creating theatre" is not the point of the exercise, or what Roy Hart Theatre technique is all about. It is definitely about technique. We were told that it teaches how to experience the extremes: in gesture, in voice, in using the space; in not holding to one image and defining it, and certainly not by explaining it. Not in holding a middle ground, well-centred, and in control. What then is this often painful process, for it is surely that into which we are thrust? We dread the moment we will have to present our text before everyone: the time when the words we have so carefully composed and rehearsed are cast before the throng and, like Pentheus resisting the Dionysian forces that are straining at his gate, are torn apart if they are not let go to see and feel the new variations calling out for expression.

I felt it myself the next to last day. The longer I held out, the weaker my text seemed. The more often I recited it to myself, the more insignificant it seemed. Trees of plenty, golf balls whizzing by, predatory birds, an Oriental girl, the Old World. I wished I had done like most of the others and taken a text written by a master and tried to bring some art along instead of some trite dream fragments that I had thought would cohere in time but which were falling farther and farther apart as time went on.

It came to this late moment when I was at last called upon. And along with me, as luck would have it, a spry dancer from home, now making a living in Paris. She is leading, and I am to keep up with her, more or less. A woman I had nearly crushed that morning in a warm-up exercise that required manipulating the rib cages of our partners to expand the inner physical space, to clear passages, to establish trust. To me she felt like a fragile bird and I a mastiff.

But no graceful or delicate movements here. She began with a comic scratching of her behind! I repeated the gesture. Again. And again. I could not help but follow, playing the clown as I do best, somehow making a parody of her movements just as her playful gestures were a parody of the serious sentiments I was trying to deliver to my intimate public. The Tree of Plenty? This felt like someone sitting on an ant-hill at a picnic, no tree in sight!

The scene changed only slightly when she began to tip-toe with the most minute steps. Of course I had to follow in lock-step...sort of. Worst of all, I couldn't get a word in edgewise without mocking my text... about magic hidden away, about wasted time, about gifts proffered, and finally about the lost worlds and values of our ancestors and what to do without them.

K. did not know my text before she began to move. The trick seemed to be, as we discovered over the course of almost two weeks, to find the moments without looking for them; as if from our most lost places we would come upon treasure we held locked inside, or demonstrated by someone across the floor from us. On a most rare occasion, a gesture shared by a host of six or eight people would convey an image and a feeling that everyone felt at once, that touched a chord that resonated in all. It could be moved into a brilliant and moving choreography or simply left alone, for a dream to bring it back again.

It took about four days for the magic moment to incubate in me. It was a few days after returning to Canada. One morning I was daydreaming about the festival and what we had and had not received from our theatrical and mythical time in Avignon. I was thinking about the moment when K. and I had drawn our duet on as long as could be endured and it was cut off just before the most dramatic passage. I was trying to imagine what it must have been like for my grandfather to have left the Old World, grown too perilous to stay on in Poland; the sacred tree I imagined him and his family gathered around, still stretching its branches to-ward the sky, as if in a desperate prayer for the future generations of his family and neighbours, many of whom would not survive the slaughter three decades later. My text concluded with sadness but also a blessing for the vaguely known forces that drive us on to unknown worlds. These words would not be heard that day, and perhaps not at all except by my partner and a few others who may have picked up the story over the two weeks, in piece-meal fashion.

Here it was four days later and it struck me: when K. was moving so nervously, so minutely, and I was looking for a moment of stillness for the majesty of the ancient tree to make its appearance, to stretch itself upward, that gesture so well known by simple folks of not so long ago, a gesture of prayer so remote for people well trained in matters of intellect and so sated with instinctual fulfilment. I realized I LOST THE MOMENT. It was there if I had decided to just stop following. To let her go on ahead, in her slow, nervous, and uncertain way, like my grandfather in America, while I stood tall, unmoving, steady as the tree of life itself, and watched her as she moved on. It might have been my grandfather's story there on the floor of the Charterhouse in Avignon, the Quebec *dançeuse* as my Zaida, and me as the gnarled old oak tree, perhaps still standing just outside a Jewish village in southern Poland. I was so disappointed I had missed the opportunity until I realized that I had captured the moment, the image, and the feeling in my memory, in my imagination. It was not lost. I can see K. and my grandfather and myself moving slowly forward from the shade of the old tree, making our way....

Even as we move away from the events of the festival, the memories will not fade away altogether: the Siberian singers sounding from the depths of endless winters; the therapist swigging wine from a bottle in the compass of the sacred well the night before the enactment of the Dionysian Mysteries; the dismembered dream the last night that brought us together back to the real world with its terrorist bombs, with a sympathetic ear to those who suffer in a world far more terrible than we would like to admit; the accordion player rejected again and again for her efforts, at last winning the crowds from the deluxe wine-tasting session with her soulful singing: a heart of gold, a bouquet of spring flowers on her table every day; lion-hearted Richard, taking his voice from the plaintive whine of a choir boy to the profound bellow of a man released at last from Circe's spell; the bullfight not attended but described with loving detail by an unlikely aficionado: the ritual I imagined would convey, more than any activity scheduled on site, the eternal battle between life and death, man and nature, instinct and art, cruelty and delicacy.

How precarious every gesture we make, and how necessary to make them with power and grace.

We return to our daily routines, back to our regular rhythms and cycles. The questions of magic still hang in the air. This time around, will we bring magic into the world by myth or song, dance or story, or will we continue our journey without the spark and intention of making the moments endure somehow by how we value them? Will we not remember them after the dissolution of the festival?

On the fourth day of the proceedings, the Italian magician saved our souls in a strange and wonderful way when he performed the simplest tricks before us. Then he related his theory of writing and put something in perspective which has had a lasting effect. He posed the parallel cases of the thief and the detective and the writer and the critic; in both situations, the action is sustained by the tension of the chase. If the critic is too clever, or if the cop is too smart, the drama is gone. His thesis was that the writer always had the power of magic in his hands to conjure a story to capture our imagination. We give it to him because we need the play in our lives; we long to suspend our disbelief. Just as we know that there are tricks in the magician's act, we cannot see them and don't really want to see them.

If the festival at times failed to create or sustain magic, it remains with us to bring the magic out into the world; from the light on the screen and the stage into the dark chambers of our hearts, and from the depths of our dreams into the light of day.

POETRY ON CASSETTE

Just Goddesses
translated and read by Charles Boer

Just Goddesses isn't only for women who like to fantasize. Sometimes men, too, desire an earful of Hera, Demeter, Aphrodite and Artemis. Charles Boer reads just the goddess myths of Greece and Rome from his intimate translations of the *Homeric Hymns* and Ovid's *Metamorphoses.* Powerful! Reassuring! Beautiful! (And just goddesses!)
2 audio tapes: 2 hrs. ISBN 1-879816-08-3 $17.95

Selected Poems of Dante
translated and read by Jay Livernois

Dante—with his journey from Hell to Heaven and everywhere in between—sang of a dreamscape only hinted at by Shakespeare's tragic heroes or Odysseus's descent to the Underworld. Jay Livernois' translation of selected cantos from Dante's epic, *The Divine Comedy,* is more exact than any to date—bold, enraging, intense—and wonderfully free of the usual poetic pieties. With notes.
2 audio tapes: 3 hrs. ISBN 1-879816-09-1 $17.95

Erotic Poems of the Earl of Rochester
read by Ian Magilton

The Earl of Rochester was Charles II's drinking pal and poet—bawdy, raucous, and yet elegant as only the rakes of the Restoration could be. His poems were long suppressed (but smart schoolboys somehow always managed to find them!). English poetry would never be so outrageous—or funny—again. The poems are read by the Obie-award winning Ian Magilton.
1 audio tape: 1 hr ISBN 1-879816-11-3 $11.95

Ovid's Metamorphoses
Translated by Charles Boer, read by Noah Pikes

Noah Pikes of the world renowned Roy Hart Theater, reads selec
Charles Boer's translation of Ovid's *Metamorphoses.* "Pike's performa:
a feel as to what the myth world of antiquity looked, thought, and acted like at
climax."—James Hillman
1 audio tape: 1 hr. ISBN 1-879816-13-X $11.95

Catullus: Selected Poems
Read by Allen Ginsberg, Translated by Jacob Rabinowitz

This bold, literal translation of the ancient Roman poet, Catullus, i:
read in delightful, hairy lines by Allen Ginsberg. Rabinowitz's
translation grasps the elegance, passion, and nastiness of 1st century
Rome, the greatest century that ever lived.
1 audio tape: 35 mins. ISBN 1-879816-03-2 $11.95

Available from:
Spring Audio
299 East Quassett Road, Woodstock, CT 06281

TWO LETTERS TO *SPRING*

To the Editors of *Spring*:

Whew! Talk about serendipity: here I am in the midst of a profound spiritual crisis, in which all that I once held sacred and esteemed seems to no longer be working in my life—I have twelve-plus years of recovery in AA, and I am a former long-time practicing Catholic—when, like cool water to a thirsting soul, your issue on "Disillusionment" [*Spring 58*] arrived. Immediately, I immersed myself in Joseph Landry's archetypal take on AA, and as I read, I realized I've connected with a kindred spirit. In many ways, Landry's experience in AA echoes my own. I, too, was a "zealous believer" who, after many years of heroin and cocaine addiction, found acceptance and renewal in AA's fellowship. I, too, however, following nearly a decade of recovery, started to question AA's most basic premises. What began as a deep conversion experience, moving from a life of violence and hopeless addiction into a fulfilling life built on simple spiritual principles, in which I also returned to my Catholic faith with a renewed vigor, eventually ended in disillusionment.

Landry's view of AA, as seen through a lens provided by archetypal psychology, helped give form to some of my own doubts about "the program." His conclusion that AA is essentially monotheistic and modeled on the Christian fall/redemption paradigm, and that the fellowship itself is secular and "depolitical" in nature, rings with truth. The seeds of my own disillusionment, too, are rooted in AA's dogmatic approach to recovery, which reflects, as Landry notes, the Christian story: "no salvation outside AA." And though salvation from addiction, or even deliverance from "demon rum," is essentially founded on timeless, universal spiritual principles—honesty, love, service—such beliefs seem hollow when they are removed from the polis. During the Persian Gulf war, for instance, the horrible reality of what was going on in that "Just War" never penetrated the AA rooms that I attended, though a few patriots proudly wore their Desert Storm tee shirts to many meetings. There was something terribly incongruous about holding hands and praying the Lord's prayer, which traditionally closes most AA meetings, with folks wearing emblems of America's war machine on their breasts. I recall, too, during the Los Angeles riots that followed the Rodney King verdict, how the meetings were weirdly disconnected from that harsh reality. Members, when mentioning the riots at all, only noted how the relentless, violent TV images that entered their living rooms "disturbed their serenity." The advice offered by long-time AA members was simple: turn off the TV and pray, and strive to clear your mind of such disturbing images.

While Landry's piece goes far in helping put my own experience into perspective, I wish he had gone further still. His account of his dissolving belief system, and how he finds himself "no longer in [the AA] story" parallels my path; however, I find myself asking, what story is he now a part of? What has replaced the recovery myth? I can't, with good conscience, totally "dis" the illusion—AA did, after all, save my life. But now I'm a man without a working belief system, an AA apostate in a lonely sort of limbo. (Unless being a born-again pagan/existential anarchist can be called a belief system.) In some ways, the depths I've reached sober are worse than my bottoming out with heroin: Now I'm feeling the psychic pain, and I'm utterly conscious of my descent. A "dis" of another sort often seems looming beyond my illusions, one that the Cumaen sibyl warned Aeneas of: "The way downward is easy from Avernus./ Black Dis's door stands open night and day./ But to retrace your steps to heaven's air,/ There is the trouble, there is the toil."

Of course, Jung offers guidance for my current situation, for he did not address himself "to the happy possessors of faith, but to those many people for whom the light has gone out, the mystery faded, and God is dead" (*CW 11*, §148). Jung understood that to many such sufferers, "there is no going back, and one does not know either whether going back is the better way." As Jung noted elsewhere, it is "only in the state of complete abandonment and loneliness that we experience the helpful powers of our own natures" (*CW 11*, §525). One might also add, hopefully, the state of disillusionment. The words of Rilke, too, offer comfort for such emptiness, for he claims, in a commentary on his Tenth Elegy—that magnificent expression of the fullest measure of human acceptance—that "this very abyss is full of the darkness of God; and where someone experiences it, let him climb down and howl away inside it (that is more necessary than crossing it)."

With a most sincere and grateful howl,
Jim Maynor
Melbourne, Florida

———

Joseph Landry replies: "Anything worth doing is worth fucking up," the late Jack M., a recovered alkie newspaperman, used to be fond of saying. If my writing posed problems without providing solutions, so be it. I'd love to come to the rescue for a man "without a working belief system," not only for the heroic value of such a move, but also because of my strong distaste for murky uncertainty. I don't think I can adequately answer Mr. Maynor's question regarding which story I am presently in. To attempt this would be comparable to asking a crab to fully describe the shell he inhabits now, without benefit of a mirror. I can't possibly see the whole thing while inside it. I can only tell you about the empty shell left back in the sand; how good it felt to have been wrapped in it, how disquieting it was when it came off, how it hurt like a sonofabitch to be without its "protection." So much for the Shell Answer Man!

Dear Joseph Landry, James A. Estep, James Hillman:

How have I loved thee, O Alcoholics Anonymous? Let me count the ways: I have feared, loved, despised, been in thrall, bored, angry; departed, with and without relapse; stayed away for long times; returned, under duress and in relief. I have been beloved, admired, respected, envied, a "star" on the speaker circuit, a sought-after sponsor, and reviled for my errant (read therapy, graduate school, hobnobbing with "normies") ways. I am "a part of"—by choice.

Existence is multiple. AA saved my life (Christian salvation), Archetypal Psychology saved my soul (Platonic re-membering). The One and the many Gods present me with no difficulty—thanks to David L. Miller—the more, the greater the Power. The problem of alcohol, for alcoholics, is digital. The soul's entanglements are analog. Why are we confused about this?

A smile of recognition overcame me with all three of your papers and letters. There has never been anything said about that program—from "it's the big teat," to "it's the greatest spiritual movement of the twentieth century"—that I do not agree with, in spite of whatever my personal threat threshold of the moment may be. The view is always just a slice.

My current slice is spoken from the vantage of 30 years study and practice of psychology, 20 of the last 21 years sober via AA, and 15 years reading Hillman and Friends.

However, I am not "well enough" to resist just this once setting the record straight for the person wanting to set the record straight. James E. stated, "No sober addict would ever, in my opinion, claim to be recovered." The title page of the big book of Alcoholics Anonymous (1955) is subtitled:

> The Story of How Many Thousands of Men and Women Have *Recovered* (italics mine) from Alcoholism

And, again, in the Forward to the First Edition:

> We, of Alcoholics Anonymous, are more than one hundred men and women who have *recovered* (italics mine) from a seemingly hopeless state of mind and body.

Non-addicts have no choice in recovery? With the possible exception of J. H., who has a largesse for being misunderstood that I can only aspire to, "normies" appear no more immune to the slings and arrows of outrageous fortune than I. We all choose.

Being unwilling to risk the loss of a quality of consciousness I've grown quite fond of (not to mention an adored husband, prosperous business, and intriguing profession), I also stay sober on the off chance that should my favorite movie star ever relapse (he has broken his anonymity in print, but nonetheless), my hand will be there when he reaches out. We can never recover.

Disillusionment? One God's betrayal is another's liberation. Having been drawn past the Santa Claus issue, I find myself willing to blithely throw over 30 years of intellectual inquiry into physics, philosophy, and psychology for one letter that begins, "Yes, Peggy, you are going to live forever." "Death is the cure for that disease that is the rage to live" (James Hiliman). And my deeper, underlying causes and conditions were and remain the rage to live. We can never recover.

The Thirteenth Step is, Leap after the Projection.

Affectionately,
Peggy Field, Ph.D.
Recovered alcoholic, recovered therapist,
                practicing citizen,
Monta Vista, California

Robert M. Stein

1924 - 1996

What's been happening?

Spring 53 (**Pagans, Christians, Jews**): Jung's secret initiation into Mithraism. James Hillman on "How Jewish is Archetypal Psychology?" Oracles. Disability. Vampires.

Spring 54 (**The Reality Issue**): Wolfgang Giegerich on killing for consciousness. Edward S. Casey on Reality. Automatic Writing. Hillman's updating of "Alchemical Blue."

Spring 55 (**The Issue from Hell**): Sheila Grimaldi-Craig's "Whipping the Chthonic Woman." "The Children of Hell." Max Nordau's *Degeneration.* "Reading Jung Backwards."

Spring 56 (**Who Was Zwingli?**): Hillman's "Once More into the Fray" takes on Wolfgang Giegrich. Benjamin Sells on Lawyer's Ethics. David Miller on Joseph Campbell. Jung's *Zarathusthra* Seminar, and the first Index to *Spring* in years!

Spring 57 (**Archetypal Sex**): Rachel Pollack on Transsexuals. Hillman on Pornography. John Haule on Erotic Analysis. Sonu Shamdasani on who really wrote Jung's memoirs.

Spring 58 (**Disillusionment**): Joseph Landry on Alcoholics Anonymous, Connie Zweig on Transcendental Meditators, David L. Hart on meeting Jung for the first time, James Hillman on the need to falsify or disguise the story of your life.

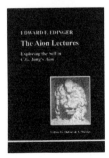